George Osborn has lived in Dorset since  retirement was a scientist. He is the auth about the county, and spent five years vis the curiosities included in *Dorset Curios* walker, and has walked extensively in the Auvergne in France, and much of souther ing the 550 mile south-west coastal path - no mean achievement for a man in his seventy-sixth year!

Frontispiece — Bere Regis Church, one of the carved figures on the nave roof (see No. 21)

Dorset Curiosities

George Osborn

THE DOVECOTE PRESS

for Gemma, Phoebe, Sadie and Thomas

First published in 1986 by The Dovecote Press Ltd
Stanbridge, Wimborne, Dorset BH21 4JD

ISBN 0 946159 38 6

© George Osborn 1986

Enlarged and reprinted 1987, 1989, 1990, 1992, 1993,1997

Phototypeset in Times by The Typesetting Bureau Ltd
Wimborne, Dorset
Printed and bound in Singapore

Contents

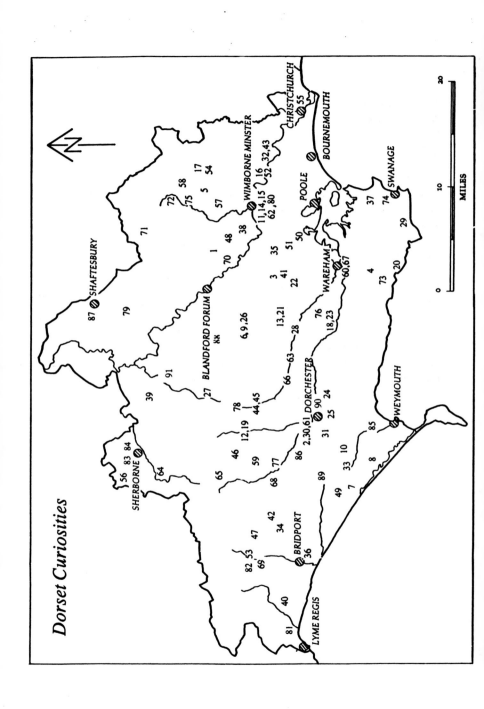

Dorset Curiosities

Introduction

Dorset has been inhabited for as long as any county in England, each
successive age leaving its mark on the landscape and adding to the legacy
that we have inherited. Many of these places and objects left behind by
our forefathers are well-known, but there are others that are not
mentioned by most guide books and do not appear on maps. I have called
them 'curiosities', because all are in some way unexpected or
extraordinary. Some of them are to be found in the remotest parts of the
county, others are in the centre of towns. Some are beautiful, some
amusing, yet more have tragic tales attached to them that give an added
poignancy to their survival. Without exception, all are undoubtedly
worth visiting.

Having derived a great deal of pleasure from finding and visiting them
myself, I have made this selection of the best of them so that others can
share my enjoyment. Not only are they remarkable in themselves, but
visiting them will mean exploring the least-crowded and most beautiful
bits of Dorset and finding out more about the county. As well as map
references, instructions on how to find them, and notes about each, I
have listed other curiosities in the area and where best to find
refreshments, so that those who wish can turn their visit into a day's
outing.

1 The Medieval Amplifiers

Position. Tarrant Rushton Church
Ordnance Map. Blandford Forum ST80/90 1.25000 (Pathfinder Series)
Map Ref. 9380/0610
Access. From Wimborne drive along the B3062 to Blandford passing
through the magnificent avenue of Beech Trees (365 on either side) until
shortly after the end of the avenue of trees you come to the ''True Lovers
Knot''. Turn right here and after about 1 mile is a turning to the right-
hand to Tarrant Rushton village. The church is at the end of the village.

Note. The two amplifiers are earthenware vessels set in the eastern face
of the chancel arch wall. They were probably placed in position about
1458 in order to amplify the voice of the priest and are the earliest known
use of jars as amplifiers in England although similar sets were installed
at Caens in France in 1432. These amplifiers at Tarrant Rushton must
have been very successful since in 1541 the Church wardens accounts of
Wimborne Minster say ''payd for 2 potts of cley for the wyndfylling of
the Church 8d''.

The church is very beautiful and unspoilt. Other objects worth looking at are the Leper Squint in the north chancel and the 2 hagioscopes. Do not miss the Lintel over the south door. It is probably the oldest thing in the church and may well date from the tenth century. The sculpture of three figures, the central one being a lamb, are as sharp today as when they came from the craftsman's hands a thousand years ago. It is almost certainly an Agnus Dei. Note also the holy water stoop still in position at the entrance to the church and the eroded mass dial on the south exterior wall. The beautiful church and charming village make this a very pleasant and interesting excursion.

Places of interest in the Neighbourhood
70. The Magnificent Hammer Beam Roof (Tarrant Crawford)
11. The Astronomical Clock (Wimborne Minster)
38. The Column which solves the meaning of Egyptian Hieroglyphs (Kingston Lacy House)

Food and Accommodation
Ample available at Wimborne

The Norman tympanum, Fordington.

2 The Norman Tympanum and the Roman Tombstone

Position. St. George's Church, Fordington (Dorchester)
Ordnance Map. Dorchester Sheet SY69 1.25 000
Map Ref. 6980/9050
Access. Fordington is a suburb of Dorchester and the church can be reached by turning left immediately after crossing the bridge as you enter Dorchester from the east.

Note. The famous Tympanum carving is to be seen over the porch door and depicts St. George on his horse aiding the Christians against the Saracens at the Battle of Antiock in 1097. This is a magnificent piece of Norman sculpture, one of the finest surviving.

   Much of Fordington is built over a Roman cemetery and an inscribed Roman tombstone, of Purbeck marble, is on view near the entrance to the church chancel. The inscription reads: '(To) Carinus, Roman citizen, (died) aged fifty years. Rufinus and Carina and Avita, his children, and Romana his wife had this set up.'

Places of interest in the Neighbourhood
30. The Room where Judge Jefferies held his Bloody Assizes (Dorchester)
61. The Hangman's Cottage (Dorchester)

Food and Accommodation
Ample available in Dorchester

3 The Beautiful Church that Hardy Saved

Position. Winterborne Tomson
Ordnance Map. Bere Regis SY89/99 1.25000
Map Ref. 8850/9740
Access. From Wimborne take the road to Dorchester (A350) for 8½ miles until you come to a red sign post. Here turn sharp right and go downhill for a quarter of a mile and take the turning to the right which leads to a small car park for the church.

Note. This beautiful little church is only 30'x20' and is dedicated to St. Andrew. The walls are 12th century. The church was for a considerable period totally deserted and neglected. Pigs and fowls wandered around it freely and the windows were broken. All seemed hopeless until the

discovery of Thomas Hardy's manuscripts in the archives of the Society for the Protection of Ancient Buildings. These were sold and the proceeds enabled the church to be restored and preserved. It is very beautiful now; plain, spotless and perfect with high pew boxes, a singing gallery, its simple screen, the pulpit and sounding board and the pretty little font. It was to the Dorset family of writers and poets, the Powys, that we are indebted for the preservation of this little gem which should not be missed.

Places of interest in the Neighbourhood
41. The Red Sign Post
22. The Ancient Hour Glass (Bloxworth)
13. The Tombstones Immortalised by Hardy (Bere Regis)
21. The Remarkable Roof (Bere Regis)

Food and Accommodation
Good food is available in two Inns in Bere Regis. Accommodation ample at Wimborne or Dorchester.

4 The Creech Folly

Position. On West Creech Hill overlooking Creech Grange
Ordnance Map. Wareham SY 88/98 1.25000
Map ref. 9130/8170
Access. From Wareham take the road to Corfe Castle as far as
Stoborough. Here take the road which turns to the right at the fork
junction. Continue on for about four miles passing directly in front of
Creech Grange and up West Creech Hill. At the top of the hill you will
see on left hand side a car park and picnic site. Leave the car here and
walk back (eastwards) along the grass track on Ridge Way Hill for about
one mile when you will see the Stone Archway on your left hand side.

Note. This stone archway is a pure folly serving no purpose other than to
provide a romantic view from Creech Grange, a view which is now lost
from the house due to the growth of Great Wood on the hillside. This
folly was built before 1746 by Denis Bond, who also was responsible for
enlarging the house. The view of Creech Grange from the folly is quite
superb.

Places of interest in the Neighbourhood
20. The Kimmeridge Folly (Kimmeridge)
25. The Hidden Church (East Lulworth)

Food and Accommodation
Freely available in Wareham

5 The Folly built by Humphrey Sturt

Position. In the parish of Horton
Ordnance Map. Bournemouth sheet 179 1.50000
Map ref. 0300/0680
Access. From Wimborne take the B3078 to Cranborne as far as the
Horton Inn which you will see on your left hand side at a crossroads
about 6 miles from Wimborne. Take the right hand fork here and

proceed to Horton Village. Here take the road to the right marked to Chalbury Common and Wimborne Minster. Go on past Manor Farm for about a mile when you will see a footpath on your left hand marked ''Bridlepath to Horton Heath''. This leads directly to the tower after about 400 yards.

Note. This tower was built as a folly by Humphrey Sturt in the early 18th century, although it has been said that he used it in old age to watch hunting when he could no longer take part. The folly has 6 storeys with brick walls. Above the fourth story the straight sides have classical pediments and the round turrets have ogee domes with ball finials: all openings have two centered heads. Inside there are beam holes for 6 floors but the woodwork has gone. The interior was used in the film of Hardy's novel *Far From the Madding Crowd* for the famous cockfighting sequence.

Places of interest in the Neighbourhood
17. The place where the would-be King was captured (Woodlands)
54. Where the Boy King sat under The Great Oak and touched for the King's Evil (Woodlands)
58. The Philosopher's Tower (Monkton up Wimborne)
75. The Sacred Circle (Knowlton)

Food and Accommodation
'Fleur de Lys' at Cranborne, offers excellent food and accommodation.

6 The Folly that Damer Built

Position. Milton Abbey School
Ordnance Map. Dorchester & Weymouth sheet 194 1.50000
Map ref. 7980/0230
Access. Park your car in the Abbey car park and take the path marked
"To Abbey". Carry on past turning off to the Abbey until you reach a
point marked "Private Road". Carry on up this road past two houses on
your right hand side. Just pass these is a Y junction. Turn right here and
you will see a five barred gate. The road from here to the Folly is through
the gateway following a pathway, until the path turns right, where you
will see the Folly on the left hand side. Unfortunately this is no longer a
right of way and permission to visit the Folly must be obtained from the
owner, who lives in the Abbey Gardens House which is just to one side.

Note. This is one of a handful of follies in Dorset and was erected by
Joseph Damer, Lord Milton, in 1790. Damer's object in building
ornamental "ruins" was to add interest to the landscape. His endeavour
to convert the Abbot's Pond into a large lake in front of his mansion had
failed, so a "ruin" in the valley with well wooded hills rising above was
his alternative. The ruins suggest a cruciform shape but are of course
incomplete and there is no roof. The Chancel is the most complete
portion of the building being 23' wide and the same length. It has two
north and two south window arches and a large east window arch. The
exterior of the east end is naturally the most imposing portion of the
building as this was the part chiefly intended to be seen. It has a lofty
octagonal pinnacle with a Latin Cross on its summit.

Places of interest in the Neighbourhood
9.. The Unique Hanging Tabernacle (Milton Abbey Church)
26. The Grass Staircase (Milton Abbey School)
27. The Crusader's Heart (Mappowder)

Food and Accommodation
Excellent meals are obtainable in Milton Abbas Village.
Accommodation ample at Blandford.

7 The Battle in the Pulpit

Position. The Church of St. Nicholas, Abbotsbury
Ordnance Map. Dorchester & Weymouth sheet 194 1.50000
Map ref. 5780/8520
Access. Abbotsbury is easily reached from Weymouth along the B3157
via Portesham.

Note. The Church of St. Nicholas is all that remains of the Benedictine
Monastery founded by Orc in the reign of Edward the Confessor. The

Abbey was destroyed at the Reformation and the stones used to build a manor house on the site next to the church. In October 1644 the parliamentary forces under Sir Anthony Ashley Cooper attacked the church and house which was defended by Captain James Strangways. After a stubborn resistance in the church and manor house the Manor was set on fire and the garrison surrendered. The Roundheads then entered the Manor to plunder but there was much gunpowder in the house which exploded, destroying the house and killing the plunderers. The battle in the church is vividly recalled by two bullet holes in the back of the Pulpit, obviously fired at a Royalist who was using the pulpit as a vantage point. Note the pre-reformation glass in the second window of south aisle showing a picture of the Virgin (late 15th century). The double fleur-de-lis in the sixth window is also 15th century. Note the beautiful Saxon carving on the west side of the tower in the churchyard.

Places of interest in the Neighbourhood
Abbotsbury. The world famous swannery first mentioned in 1393, the great Abbey Barn (272' x 31'), St. Catherine's Chapel (late 14th century), the sub-tropical gardens, Abbotsbury Castle (an iron-age earthwork 1½ miles north-west of church).
8.   The Ancient Stone Cross (Langton Herring)
33. The Man who was Buried Neither in the Church or out of it (Portesham)
49. The Tranquil Ruined Chapel Hidden in a Coppice (Abbotsbury)

Food and Accommodation
Excellent meals are obtainable at 'the Ilchester Arms' and the 'Swan'. Accommodation freely available in Dorchester.

8 The Ancient Stone Cross

Position. At Langton Herring
Ordnance Map. Dorchester & Weymouth sheet 194 1.50000
Map ref. 6250/8240
Access. Take the B3157 from Weymouth as far as the turning into
Langton Herring which is at a point called Langton Cross (about 4 miles
from Weymouth). Immediately at the commencement of the road to the
village you will see the stone cross on the right, standing alone in land
that has recently been cleared.

Note. This fine old Latin cross was hewn out of one solid block of
Portland Ridgeway stone and is firmly embedded in the ground. Judging
from the bold chamfered edges both to the shaft and the arms and the
general design the cross is probably 14th century. It will be noticed that
the top or head of the cross has been broken off and the arms somewhat
damaged and the whole weather-worn. No inscription or lettering can be
found. The height above ground to where it is broken off is 3'2" and it is
embedded in the ground 1'7". The shaft at the base is 11" square. The
chamfering is unusually bold and measures 2¾". The cross faces south
and before the deeply excavated road to Portesham was made, it would
have stood up much more prominently than it does at present. There is
no clue as to the history of this very ancient cross but it is on the direct
route from Weymouth to the Monastery at Abbotsbury and may have
been a marker to pilgrims.

Places of interest in the Neighbourhood
Abbotsbury. The world famous Swannery first mentioned in 1393, the
great Abbey Barn (272' x 31'), St. Catherine's Chapel (late 14th
century), the sub-tropical gardens, Abbotsbury Castle (an iron-age
earthwork 1½ miles north-west of church).
  7. The Battle in the Pulpit (Abbotsbury)
33. The Man who was Buried Neither in the Church or out of it
(Portesham)
49. The Tranquil Ruined Chapel Hidden in a Coppice (Abbotsbury)

Food and Accommodation
Excellent food and drink at the 'Elm Tree Inn', Langton Herring.
Accommodation, plenty available at Weymouth

9 The Unique Hanging Tabernacle

Position. Milton Abbey Church, the Presbytery
Ordnance Map. Dorchester & Weymouth sheet 194 1.50000
Map ref. 7980/0230
Access. There is a special car park allocated to visitors to the Abbey. From here it is a short well-signposted walk to the Abbey Church.

Note. From earliest time the Catholic Church has always kept the consecrated host in a tabernacle, usually on the altar, believing it to be the body of Christ. Sometimes, however, the host is kept in a separate

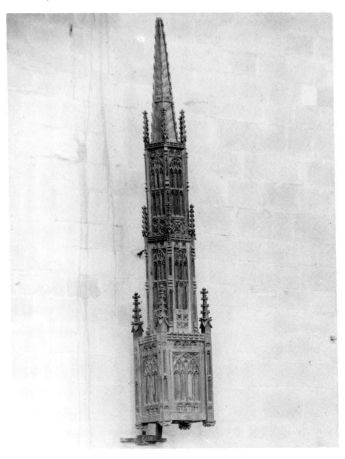

tabernacle, as was the case at Milton Abbey where it was preserved in a hanging pyx-shrine. The oak shrine is superbly carved and is of three stages and a spire, from whose apex it was originally suspended. The pyx-shrine is unique, for no other examples in this country escaped destruction during the Reformation.

Places of interest in the Neighbourhood
  6. The Folly that Damer Built (Milton Abbey School)
26. The Grass Staircase (Milton Abbey School)
27. The Crusader's Heart (Mappowder)

Food and Accommodation
Refreshments are available in Milton Abbas village. Accommodation is available at Blandford.

10 The Altar Stone the Reformers Missed

Position. The Chapel of St. Bartholomew, Corton (Portesham)
Ordnance Map. Weymouth (North) SY 68/78
Map ref. 6370/8550
Access. This is not the easiest of places to find but it is very well worth the effort. The best approach is from Dorchester along the Old Roman road to Weymouth as far as Upwey. Here take the road to Martinstown and after a mile turn off to the left along the road to Portesham. Continue on through the hamlet of Friar Waddon and shortly afterwards you will see a sign to Corton Farm. Follow the track down hill as far as the farm house. The Chapel is just beyond and open to the public.

Note. The chapel is quite unique in that it contains the only, as far as is known, pre-Reformation Altar Stone still in position. At the Reformation in 1550 an act of Edward VI was passed whereby all altar stones which every church had for the saying of Mass were to be thrown out of the church and destroyed. In many cases the stones were hidden by Catholics in the hope of better times, and a few have been found and lovingly restored. At Corton alone, however, the stone was left intact and is still to be seen where it has stood since the building of the chapel in the thirteenth century.

The probable explanation of how this altar stone escaped destruction is that the chapels were suppressed and their revenues taken away by the Chantry Act of 1547, whereas the order to remove the stone altars was issued in 1550, three years later. As the chapels by then were closed for public worship the order did not effect them and Corton in this very remote spot was left in peace, forgotten by the reformers. In 1552 the whole of the ornaments then in the chapel, namely a chalice, one vestment of blue velvet, one bell, one surplice and two table cloths were removed and nothing was left for the service in the chapel. Unfortunately at the present time the beautiful stone altar has a wooden covering which detracts from its beauty, and it is to be hoped that this will be one day removed so that the altar may be seen in its full glory.

Place of interest in the Neighbourhood
  8. The Ancient Stone Cross (Langton Herring)
31. The Flying Angel (Winterbourne Steepleton)
33. The Man who was buried neither in the church nor out of it (Portesham)

Food and Accommodation
At Portesham good meals may be obtained at the 'Kings Arms'.
The ''Honey Pot'' offers excellent cream teas during the summer.

11 The Ancient Astronomical Clock

Position. In Wimborne Minster, on the south wall of the baptistry
Ordnance Map. Bournemouth (west) sheet SZ09 1.25000
Map Ref. 0090/9980

Note. This famous clock was built in about 1320, long before Copernicus
showed that the earth moves round the sun. In consequence the earth is
the centre, round which the sun, moon and the stars all revolve. The sun
in the outer circle represents the hour hand; the moon on the middle
circle marks the phases of the lunar month and the earth is fixed in the
centre. It is a twenty-four hour clock and is still accurate after nearly
seven centuries. The sides are Elizabethan. It was redecorated in 1979
faithfully copying old designs discovered under layers of paint. It was
made by Peter Lightfoot, a monk of Glastonbury, who made three other
such clocks, one of which survives in Wells Cathedral.

Places of interest in the Neighbourhood
14. The Man in the Wall (Wimborne)
15. The Leper Hospital (Wimborne)
62. The Chained Library (Wimborne)

Food and Accommodation
The Kings Head in The Square offers excellent accommodation, and
there are numerous restaurants and public houses which offer good fare.

12 The Madonna that Escaped the Reformation

Position. Cerne Abbas, in the tower of the Parish Church of St. Mary
Ordnance Map. Cerne Abbas. Sheet ST60 1.25000
Map Ref. 6660/0120

Note. In Catholic times the people of England had a great devotion to the
Virgin Mother, and in almost all Parish Churches there was a statue of
the Madonna and Child in a niche in the tower above the porch. During
the Reformation many such statues were pulled from their niches, wall
paintings were whitewashed, stained glass was smashed, altar stones
thrown out, rood screens removed. What little was left of the glory of
pre-Reformation churches was finally destroyed when the ultra-
protestants under Cromwell were let loose and went around destroying
anything of beauty they could find. Yet somehow despite all this the
Madonna and Child remained in their niche in the tower of Cerne Parish
Church. How it escaped the fury of the iconoclasts is a mystery; it is
probably one of a few out of many thousand to survive.

Places of interest in the Neighbourhood
19. The Well St Augustine Made (Cerne Abbas churchyard)
    The Cerne Giant

Food and Accommodation
Ample food and accommodation are available in Cerne Abbas Village

13 The Tombstones Immortalised by Hardy

Position. Bere Regis Church; South Aisle
Ordnance Map. Bere Regis SY89 1.25000
Map Ref. 8470/9480

Note. The Burial Vault of the Turbevilles is under the floor of the south aisle and a Brass of Sir Robert Turbeville, Lord of the Manor under Henry VIII, is on the wall next to an altar tomb of the Turbevilles. The Turbevilles were a very ancient family coming over with the Normans and for several centuries shared the neighbouring estates with the nuns from Tarrant Abbey. At the dissolution of the Monastaries all the Abbey lands came to the Turbevilles who however remained faithful to the ancient faith. Hardy knew these tombs well and used them as the central point of *Tess of the D'Urbevilles*, when the parson told Tess's father, a farm labourer, that he was descended from the noble family so beginning the sad path that led to the tragedy of Tess. Thus to these tombs we owe one of the best loved books in the English language.

Places of interest in the Neighbourhood
21. The Remarkable Roof (Bere Regis)
22. The Ancient Hour Glass (Bloxworth)
41. The Red Sign Post
 3. The Beautiful Church that Hardy Saved (Winterborne Tomson)

Food and Accommodation
Good food is available at two inns at Bere Regis. Accommodation at Wimborne and Dorchester.

14 The Man in the Wall

Position. Wimborne Minster, in a recess in the south wall of Trinity Chapel
Ordance Map. Bournemouth (West). Sheet SZ09 1.25000
Map Ref. 0090/9980

Note. Anthony Ettrick (1622-1703) was a native of Wimborne and had a distinguished career as a lawyer and was at one time Recorder of Poole. According to legend, Ettrick was so offended with the inhabitants of Wimborne that he made a solemn protest that he would not be buried within their church nor out of it, neither below ground nor above it. Later his anger cooled, and using his skill as a lawyer he endeavoured to evade breaking his oath by obtaining permission to make the recess in the wall where his coffin is placed - neither within the church or yet within the churchyard and where the surface of the ground outside would be neither

above or below it.

In his old age Ettrick became more eccentric and finally was convinced that he would die in 1691 and had the coffin made with that date inscribed on it. When he finally died in 1703 the date had to be altered as can be plainly seen. For many years it was believed that Ettrick was actually buried in the tomb but a careful examination in 1857 showed that his relations had buried him under the coffin. He left twenty shillings a year to keep his coffin painted in good order and this has been honoured.

Places on interest in the Neighbourhood
11. The Ancient Astronomical Clock (Wimborne Minster)
15. The Leper Hospital (Wimborne)
62. The Chained Library (Wimborne Minster)

Food and Accommodation
'The Kings Head' in The Square offers excellent accommodation, and there are numerous restaurants and public houses which offer good fare.

15 The Leper Hospital

Position. At Wimborne on the Badbury Rings-Blandford Road (B3082) about 1 mile from the centre of town and at the point where there is a turn-off to Cowgrove.
Ordnance Map. Bournemouth Sheet 179 1.50000
Map Ref. 0040/0030

Note. This Chapel of St Margaret and St Antony dates from the early 13th century and was built as the Chapel of the Leper Hospital. Leprosy is known to have existed in England as far back at the 10th century. It was probably introduced by pilgrims returning from the Holy Land or by traders from the East. Its spread was due to insanitary conditions and to an excessive use of salted food. This Chapel was here in the reign of King John and measures 38' x 13'. The Pope of the time granted an Indulgence of a year to anyone contributing to its building or to its maintenance. Unfortunately the Chapel was badly restored in recent years and the magnificent 13th century wall paintings obliterated by an architect who thought them to be Victorian! As far as is known this is the only leper hospital left in the county to remind us of those grim days when lepers were a frequent sight on the roads.

Places of interest in the Neighbourhood
11. The Ancient Astonomical Clock (Wimborne Minster)
14. The Man in the Wall (Wimborne Minster)
62. The Chained Library (Wimborne Minster)

Food and Accommodation
'The Kings Head' in The Square offers excellent accommodation, and there are numerous restaurants and public houses which offer good fare.

16 The Mystery of the Jesuit Tombs

Position. Hampreston Church
Ordnance Map. Bournemouth. Sheet 179. 1.50000
Map Ref. 0050/9890
Access. From Wimborne take the A31 eastwards for one mile. Then at a
Y junction take right fork (B3073), after about ½ mile there is a signpost
to Hampreston.

Note. In the centre of the aisle at All Saints Church two tombstones are
laid side by side in a place of honour. The first reads ''Here lieth ye body
of Mr. Caryll S. J. Feb ye 18th 1750. R.I.P,'' and the second reads
''Here lieth ye body of Mr Charles Caryll S. J. who dyd ye 12 day of
June 1745. R.I.P.'' Now the memorials are clearly those of Jesuit
Priests and this was a time of intense persecution of Catholic priests,
especially Jesuits, yet here two are laid to rest in a place of honour in a
Protestant Church. The priests themselves, who were cousins, were
members of the staunchly Catholic family the Carylls of West Grinstead
in Sussex. It is known that the Jesuits had a house nearby at Stapehill
(now Stapehill Abbey) and presumably the two priests had lived and
worked there. That they were buried in Hampreston Church is probably
due to the fact that the living was in the hands of the great Catholic
family the Arundell's of Wardour Castle and presumably they had appointed a parson who was tolerant of Catholicism in those intolerant
days and he may well have been friendly with the Jesuits of Stapehill.

Places of interest in the Neighbourhood
11. The Ancient Astronomical Clock (Wimborne Minster)
14. The Man in the Wall (Wimborne Minster)
15. The Leper Hospital (Wimborne Minster)
32. The Strange Case of the Modest Lady of Lydlinch (West Parley)
43. The Gibbet that became a Sun Dial (West Parley)

Food and Accommodation
Ample available at Wimborne

17 The Place Where the Would-Be King was Captured

Position. In a field on Monmouth Ash Farm, Woodlands
Ordnance Map. Bournemouth. Sheet 179 1.50000
Map Ref. 0700/0600
Access. From Wimborne take the B3078 Cranbourne Road. After about 6 miles you will see the ''Horton Inn'' at a crossroad. Take the turning on the right hand and drive via Horton for about 4 miles until you come to Clump Hill where a road on the right hand side leads to Mannington. Immediately opposite is an unmade road which is a right of way. Leave car here and walk half a mile as far as Monmouth Ash Farm on left hand side. There is no right of way to the site of the Monmouth Ash but permission to cross the two fields to the site is readily given if the farmer

James, Duke of Monmouth.

is approached. The track from the farmhouse leads to some derelict buildings beyond which are two fields. The Ash under which Monmouth was found lying in the ditch is in the second field, halfway along the hedge on the left hand side, and there is a plaque nailed to the tree to record the event.

Note. The Duke of Monmouth was the illegitimate son of Charles II by his mistress Lucy Walters. He had no valid claim to the throne but he gambled on the protestants dislike of James II, a Catholic. So in 1685 he landed at Lyme Regis and raised about six thousand followers. At Sedgemoor his untrained mob was easily defeated by the Royal troops and Monmouth fled, first towards London. At Woodyates he realised the road to London was blocked so he turned with one companion and tried to cross the fields to Poole. The whole countryside was looking for him and he had to find shelter for the night in a ditch under the Ash tree, where he was captured on the morning of July 8th, cold and starving. In his pockets the would-be king had only a handful of raw peas and the badge of the order of the Garter given to him by Charles II. He was taken to London and executed for high treason. It is very moving to stand at the exact spot where he had lain hidden all night in fear of his life. The present Ash tree replaced the original one which died of old age, but is in the exact spot.

Places of interest in the Neighbourhood
  5. The Folly that Humphrey Sturt Built, Horton Tower (Horton)
54. Where the Boy King sat under the Great Oak (Woodlands)
58. The Philosopher's Tower (Monkton up Wimborne)

Food and Accommodation
Available at the Fleur de Lys Cranborne, ample also available at Wimborne.

18 The Grave of a Hero

Position. In village graveyard at Moreton
Ordnance Map. Wareham. Sheet 88/98 1.25000
Map Ref. 8040/8940
Access. At Wool take the small road to the right on the north side of the
railway crossing when approaching from Wareham. This road leads
directly to Moreton Village where you will easily find the graveyard.

Note. Here lie the mortal remains of T. E. Lawrence, (Lawrence of
Arabia), soldier, writer, man of heroism and mystery. Lawrence had
come to Dorset in 1923 in order to escape from his fame, buying
''Cloud's Hill'', the Moreton cottage he was living in at the time of his
fatal motorbike accident in 1935. His grave lies in a peaceful setting that
provides an unlikely contrast with the violence he had so often
witnessed. The only claim to fame on the headstone is the inscription
'Fellow of All Souls Oxford'.

Place of interest in the Neighbourhood
76. Cloud's Hill (Bovington)
23. The Church with the Beautiful Engraved Windows (Moreton)

Food and Accommodation
None at Moreton, but available at Wool.

19 The Well of St Augustin

Position. In the churchyard at Cerne Abbas
Ordnance Map. Cerne Abbas. Sheet ST60 1.25000
Map Ref. 6660/0120
Access. Walk up the beautiful street which leads to the Abbey gateway
and just beyond the pond on your right hand side there is a small iron
gateway which leads to the churchyard. Pass through the gateway and
follow the path directly in front of you with the churchyard on your left.
After about 100 yards you will see the Well with Spring Water gushing
continuously into it.

Note. Legend has it that St Augustin made this well when he visited
Cerne on his great mission to convert the English in the 6th century.
Local tradition claims curative properties for the well. On the other hand
no direct evidence exists to support the theory and writing centuries later
William of Malmesbury refers to it as the ''Silver Well''. Whatever the
truth it is very ancient and well worth a visit. The partial covering of the
well with stones probably means that sick people lay in it hoping to be
cured.

Places on interest in the Neighbourhood
12. The Madonna that escaped the Fury of the Reformers (Cerne Abbas)

Food and Accommodation
Ample accommodation and food available in Cerne Abbas Village.

20 The Kimmeridge Folly

Position. On cliff top overlooking Kimmeridge Bay
Ordnance Map. Purbeck. Sheet SY 87/97/SZ07 1.25000
Map Ref. 9090/7870
Access. From the car park on beach walk eastwards following the
Coastal Path. A flight of steps up the hill leads directly to the Folly.

Note. This folly, called Clavel's Tower, was built in 1831 by the Rev.
John Richards who took the name of Clavel on inheriting Smedmore
House and Estate in 1817.

The tower is circular, and the first stage is surrounded by a colonnade
for which the basement forms a projecting podium. It is now in a
dangerous state and badly in need of repair. The view from the Folly on a
fine day looking over the bay and cliffs running westward is quite superb.

Places of interest in the Neighbourhood
  4. Creech Folly (West Creech Hill)
73. Where the Stars and Stripes Began (Steeple)

Food and Accommodation
Available at Kimmeridge, in the summer, but plenty available in Corfe
Castle and Wareham.

21 The Remarkable Roof

Position. Bere Regis Church
Ordnance Map. Bere Regis. SY89 1.25000
Map Ref. 8470/9480

Note. This very remarkable and beautiful roof was constructed between 1475 and 1500 AD to the order of Cardinal Morton, who was born at Milton Stileham. The central bosses on the trusses represent Cardinal Morton, his coat of arms and various symbols associated with him including the Tudor Rose. The twelve life size figures (two on each truss) represent the twelve apostles. On the north side left to right are Andrew Bartholomew, James 1, James 2, John, Judas. On the south side, left to right are Lebbaeus, Matthew, Phillip, Simon Peter, Simon Zelotes, Thomas. The carvings are strongly coloured and the whole roof is in a fine state of preservation and quite unique.

Places of interest in the Neighbourhood
   3. The beautiful church which Hardy saved (Winterborne Tomson
 13. The Tombstones Immortalised by Hardy (Bere Regis Church)
 22. The Ancient Hour Glass (Bloxworth)
 41. The Red Sign Post (Anderson)

Food and Accommodation
Good food is available at the Inns in Bere Regis, but accommodation must be sought at either Wimborne or Dorchester.

22 The Ancient Hour Glass

Position. The Parish Church at Bloxworth
Ordnance Map. Bere Regis. Sheet SY89 1.25000
Map Ref. 8810/9470
Access. Take the road from Wimborne to Dorchester (A31) for about 8½
miles as far as the Red Sign Post. Turn left here, proceed for about 1 mile
and take right fork at junction. This will lead you directly to Bloxworth
Village where the Church is easily visible.

Note. The hour glass still to be seen in the Jacobean pulpit is the sole
reminder of a remarkable age when, following the banishing of the Mass
as the central act of Christian worship, the Sermon replaced it and
preachers would preach to captive audiences (attendance was obligatory
to all) for at least an hour. If at the end of the hour the parson turned the
hour glass over the congregation knew they were in for another hour of
preaching! This hour glass at Bloxworth is the only one left in Dorset
from these times. Unfortunately it no longer works because a verger
gave it an unlucky blow in 1868 when the Chancel was being restored.

Places of interest in the Neighbourhood
  3. The beautiful Church that Hardy saved (Winterborne Tomson)
41. The Red Sign Post (Anderson)
Bloxworth Manor House. One of the most beautiful manor houses in the
county. Now beautifully restored and open occasionally in the summer;
it was used as the main house in the film *Far from the Madding Crowd*.

Food and Accommodation
Ample available at Wimborne and Dorchester

23 The Church with the Beautiful Engraved Windows

Position. Moreton
Ordnance Map. Dorchester/Weymouth. Sheel 194 1.50000
Map Ref. 8060/8930
Access. From Wool take the road on the north side of the railway crossing westwards and continue along for about 2½ miles until you reach the tiny hamlet of Moreton. The Church lies inside the grounds of Moreton House, but is clearly marked and open to the public. It stands in a parkland of great beauty.

Note. The Church was rebuilt in 1733 by William Frampton and yet again in 1766 by James Frampton. In the 1840's considerable alterations and extensions were made but it is still a fine example of 18th century architecture. In October 1940 the Church suffered very severe damage when a bomb from a German raider fell in the churchyard close to the north wall. The north wall was destroyed and all the windows were shattered to pieces. The Church was gradually rebuilt using the original stone wherever possible and re-opened in 1950. The glory of the restoration is the glass engravings on every window by Laurence Whistler. These are very beautiful and quite unique and well worth travelling many miles to see. A small guide obtainable at the Church gives details of the engravings.

Places of interest in the Neighbourhood
18. The Grave of a Hero (Moreton)
76. Clouds Hill (Moreton)

Food and Accommodation
None available at Moreton, but plenty at Wool and Wareham.

our father & mother

Sybil Findlay

1872-1959

24 The Church which Parson Barnes Loved

Position. Whitcombe. Halfway between Dorchester and Broadmayne (A352)
Ordnance Map. Dorchester and Weymouth. Sheet 194 1.50000
Map Ref. 7170/8840

Note. This very ancient and beautifully restored Church dates from Saxon times, as is shown by two late 10th century Saxon Crosses which are to be seen on the steps of the Rood Screen. The wall frescoes are of outstanding merit. To the west of the blocked Norman door is a painted arcade of trefoiled niches dating about 1300. The beautiful frescoes of St Christopher on the other side of the door are a hundred years later and show the Saint wading westwards with one hand on a large staff, and the other pulling his robe out of the water. Christ as a child sits on his shoulders. Note the mermaid combing her hair and holding a mirror.

This is one of the finest St Christopher frescoes that I have seen in a lifetime of visiting old Churches. In 1847 Colonel Damer of Came House presented William Barnes, the Dorset dialect poet, with the donative (rather less than a curacy) of Whitcombe with a stipend of £13 a year when Barnes was a school master at Dorchester. Here he preached his first sermon and in February 1885 he gave his last sermon in this lovely place. His daughter wrote ''Father was driven over to Whitcombe and took the last service he was able to take''. In the same little church in which his ministry began, there he ended it.

Places of interest in the Neighbourhood
  2. The Norman Typanum and the Roman tombstone (Dorchester)
30. The Room where Judge Jefferies held his Bloody Assizes
      (Dorchester)
61. The Hangman's Cottage (Dorchester)

25 The Sad Story of Mary Channing

Position. Dorchester on the Weymouth Road, A354.
Ordnance Map. Dorchester and Weymouth. Sheet 194. 1.50000
Map Ref. 89.50/6900

Note. On the left hand side as you leave Dorchester along the Weymouth road you will see the Roman Amphitheatre, one of the finest examples of its kind still extant. It was originally a sacred circle built in Neolithic times, c. 2000 B.C., and converted by the Romans in about 100 A.D. as a centre for their games. In the late 17th century and throughout most of the 18th century it was the site for executions and upon this spot many must have suffered the cruel lingering death by strangling that our murderous laws condemned man, woman or child, even for a theft of 5 shillings in value. It is shown in the illustration below in the usual pattern of two uprights with a crossbeam connecting them; the drawing shows space enough between the uprights to allow a two wheel cart to pass between; the cart that bore the victim and his coffin. Crowds of up to 10,000 used to gather here to watch the executions and they did so much damage to the earthworks that in 1795 the gallows were transferred to the new prison in the town.

The most famous execution on the old site was that of Mary Channing in 1705 at the age of 19. When a mere girl she was forced by her parents

to marry Richard Channing a grocer of Dorchester. Her life with him was dull for her heart was elsewhere and she longed to be free; at last she poisoned him by giving him white mercury, first in rice milk and then in a glass of wine. She was found guilty and condemned to death but pleaded pregnancy. She was removed to prison and eighteen weeks after the birth she was dragged to the gallows protesting loudly all the way that she was innocent. At the gallows she found a crowd of over ten thousand who had come to watch the dreadful scene as she was first strangled and then burnt.

Places of interest in the Neighbourhood
  2. The Norman Tympanum.
30. The Room where Judge Jefferies held his bloody Assize.
61. The Hangman's Cottage.
31. The Flying Angel.
24. The Church which Parson Barnes loved.

Food and Accommodation
Ample at Dorchester.

26 The Grass Staircase

Position. In the grounds of Milton Abbey School
Ordnance Map. Dorchester and Weymouth. Sheet 194 1.50000
Map Ref. 7980/0230
Access. Leave your car in the visitors car park and follow path marked
"To Abbey". Keep along this path until you see the grass staircase on
your left hand side.

Note. The staircase consists of one hundred and eleven steps of turf
between solid balustrades of yew. At the top of this long flight of steps is
a chapel originally built by the Saxons but rebuilt in the 12th century by
the Normans. Legend has it that the chapel, dedicated to St. Catherine, is
on the site where Athelstan, first King of all England, camped with his
guards on their way north to meet the Danes and here he dreamt he
would be victorious. The Anglo-Saxon Chronicle tells us the dream
came true and that Athelstan founded Milton Abbey in thanksgiving for
his victory and also for the soul of his brother Edwin in whose death he
had been implicated. It is not possible to use the steps to visit the Chapel
but there is a special path some distance back which leads to the Chapel.

Places of interest in the Neighbourhood
   6. The Folly that Damer Built (Milton Abbey School)
   9. The Unique Hanging Tabernacle (Milton Abbey Church)
 27. The Crusader's Heart (Mappowder)

Food and Accommodation
Refreshments are available in Milton Abbas Village. Accommodation is
available at Blandford.

27 The Crusader's Heart

Position. In the Church of Mappowder
Ordnance Map. Dorchester and Weymouth. Sheet 194 1.50000
Map Ref. 7350/0600
Access. Mappowder is not very easy to find, the best route is probably from Milton Abbas to Hilton, Ansty Cross, Higher Ansty, then to Mappowder, where the church is clearly visible.

Note. In the recess in the south wall, obviously made to receive it, is an effigy made in Caen Stone of a knight in thirteenth century chain mail and surcoat with sword and shield. His head rests on a cushion, his feet on a lion and he holds a heart in his hands. The effigy is only eighteen inches long and this has led to the legend of a boy crusader being buried here. In fact it is the heart burial of a knight who had died on Crusade is Palestine and whose heart had been embalmed and sent to his home in Dorset. The knight was probably a member of the Coker family and his crossed legs indicate that he had died in action.

Places of interet in the Neighbourhood
  6. The Folly that Damer Built (Milton Abbey School)
  9. The Unique Hanging Tabernacle (Milton Abbey Church)
  26. The Grass Staircase (Milton Abbey School)

Food and Accommodation
The nearest town for food and accommodation is Blandford.

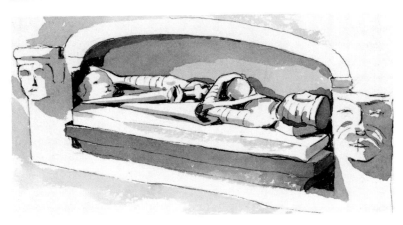

28 The Beautiful War Memorial

Position. Briantspuddle
Ordnance Map. Bere Regis SY89/99 1.25000
Map Ref. 8140/9340
Access. From Bere Regis take the A35 to Dorchester for about 2 miles
when you will see a sign post on your left hand side marked
Briantspuddle. Go down the road to the village (1 mile) and at the
crossroads take the road to the right. After a few hundred yards you will
see the memorial.

Note. The memorial carved by one of the finest sculptors of the 20th century, Eric Gill, consists of a tall cross with a life size statue of the wounded Christ on the north side and on the south side there is a Madonna and child under a canopy. This surely must be one of the most beautiful war memorials in England, and one can only be grateful that this remote village had the vision to have so superb a memorial made.

Places of interest in the Neighbourhood
  3. The Beautiful Church that Hardy Saved (Winterborne Tomson)
13. The Tombstone Immortalised by Hardy (Bere Regis)
21. The Remarkable Roof (Bere Regis)
22. The Ancient Hour Glass (Bloxworth)
41. The Red Sign Post (Anderson)

Food and Accommodation
Food available at Bere Regis, accommodation in Dorchester.

The gravestones of Benjamin Jesty and his wife, Elizabeth.

[54]

29 The Tomb of the Man who Discovered Innoculation

Position. In the Churchyard at Worth Matravers
Ordnance Map. Purbeck. Sheet 87/97/SZ07 1.25000
Map Ref. 9730/7750

Note. In the eighteenth century smallpox was rife in England and killed thousands of people every year. Farmer Benjamin Jesty, who lived in this lovely village, noted that cowmen and dairymaids seldom if ever caught smallpox and reasoned that it was probably due to the fact that they had suffered the much milder cowpox which made them immune to the deadly smallpox. Using a knitting needle he gave his family cowpox, and was thus the first man to try innoculation some twenty years before the more famous Dr Jenner began to practise it. The discovery of innoculation has saved countless millions of human lives all over the world and its unlikely discovery in this remote village was all due to the courage and intelligence of Benjamin Jesty, whose tomb can be seen in the pleasant churchyard.

Places of interest in the Neighbourhood
 4. The Creech Folly (West Creech Hill)
20. The Kimmeridge Folly (Kimmeridge)
25. The Hidden Church (East Lulworth)
73. Where the Stars and Stripes Began (Steeple)

Food and Accommodation
'The Square and Compass' at Worth Matravers offers good food and drink. For accommodation the 'Scott Arms' at Kingston is very good.

30 The Room where Judge Jefferies held his Bloody Assize

Position. At the Antelope Hotel, Dorchester in the Oak Room
Ordnance Map. Dorchester and Weymouth. Sheet 194 1.50000
Map Ref. 6960/9070
Access. Go through the arched gateway to the hotel and on to the end of
the yard where there is a sign ''Oak Room''. Go up the steps which lead
you to the Court Room. This room was the only room in Dorchester at
the time large enough to hold the trial and is today almost as it was when
on September 5th, 1685 Judge Jefferies opened the so called ''Bloody
Assizes''.

Note. Judge Jefferies was trying some 340 prisoners who had been
arrested in the wake of the Monmouth Rebellion and the Duke of
Monmouth's defeat at the Battle of Sedgemoor. By the time the Assize

moved on 74 men had been hanged, 175 condemned to transportation, 55 pardoned and a further 30 either remanded in custody or set free for lack of evidence.

Places of interest in the Neighbourhood
2. The Norman Tympanum and the Roman Tombstone (Fordington Church)
7. The Battle in the Pulpit (Abbotsbury)
31. The Flying Angel (Winterbourne Steepleton)
49. The Ruined Chapel Hidden in a Coppice (Abbotsbury)
61. The Hangman's Cottage (Dorchester)

Food and Accommodation
Ample available in Dorchester, and at the Antelope Hotel itself.

31 The Flying Angel

Position. Winterbourne Steepleton Church
Ordnance Map. Dorchester and Weymouth. Sheet 194 1.50000
Map Ref. 6290/8999
Access. From Dorchester take the A35 road to Bridport for a couple of
miles when you will see a turning marked Martinstown. Take the road to
this village and continue straight on for about a mile to Winterbourne
Steepleton.

Note. Built into the South Wall of the church is a Saxon sculpture of
international reputation dated by Pevsner to the tenth century. It is
beautifully carved in high relief. Hutchins (2nd edit) says of it "The
figure wears a monkish habit and is in a half-recumbent position. It may
have formed a representation of St Michael (Patron of the Church)
thrusting Satan out of heaven. The head is uncovered and the features
are well and sharply chisselled". From this description it would appear
that the stone must have occupied an inverted position when Hutchins
saw it in the late 18th century. The figure, in fact, evidently represents a

flying angel, the interior upper angle of the front wing having been chopped off. The rather loose outer garment reaching down to the knees has several folds crossing the chest which have been mistaken for chains. From the knees to the angles extends an inner loose gown. Between the wings and the body is a floating garment, the extremity of which forms a fold of peculiar shape common in the garments represented in illuminations and sculptures of the tenth century. The right arm is entirely broken off, the left arm is however partially shown and bent upwards at the elbow. The feet are naked. The stone is about twenty-five inches long and sixteen inches high.

Places of interest in the Neighbourhood
2. The Norman Tympanum and the Roman Tombstone (Fordington Church)
7. The Battle in the Pulpit (Abbotsbury)
30. The Room Where Judge Jefferies held his Bloody Assizes (Dorchester)
49. The Ruined Chapel Hidden in a Coppice (Abbotsbury)
61. The Hangman's Cottage (Dorchester)

Food and Accommodation
Ample available at Dorchester and Portesham.

32 The Strange Case of the Modest Lady of Lydlinch

Position. Church of Lydlinch and Church at West Parley
Ordnance Map. For Lydlinch: Sturminster Newton. Sheet ST71 1.25000
Map Ref. 7440/1340
Ordnance Map. For West Parley: Bournemouth West. Sheet SZ09
1.25000
Map Ref. 0870/9680

Note. This strange story had two locations because the unknown lady of the 14th century was said to have been the Lady of the Manor of West Parley who on her marriage was compelled by her husband to live at Lydlinch. She said on her death bed that as her heart was in West Parley in life she wished it to be buried there. The heart was buried in a 14th century urn under a circular stone. The urn was excavated in 1895 and now can be seen resting on the stone behind an iron grille on the outside east wall. The body was buried in a tomb directly outside the entrance to Lydlinch Church with the following inscription:

> Here lie the remains of a lady
> who gave to the rector of this
> church for ever one portion of
> tyths arising out of Dudsbury Farm
> in West Parley and another out of
> Knowle Farm in Woodlands.

She must have been very modest, because she left no reference to her name either at West Parley or Lydlinch.

Places of interest in the Neighbourhood
16. The Mystery of the Jesuit Tombs (Hampreston Church)
43. The Gibbet that became a Sun Dial (West Parley Church)
52. The Woman who did What she Could (Hampreston Church)
55. The Empty Tomb and the Tragic Countess (Christchurch Priory)

Food and Accommodation
Ample available at Christchurch.

33 The Man Who Was Buried Neither in the Church or Out of it

Position. Portesham Church
Ordnance Map. Weymouth (North) Sheet SY 68/78 1.25000
Map Ref. 6025/8580

Note. On the south wall is a tomb with one half outside the church and

the other half inside. It is the tomb of William Weare and the epitaph reads:

> William Weare lies here in dust
> As thou and I and all men must
> Once plundered by Sabean force
> Some cald it war but others worse
> With confidence he pleads his cause
> And kings to be above these laws
> September's eyghth day died hee
> When near the date of 63

Anno Domini 1670

Weare expressed his last wish to be buried neither in the church nor out of the church and his wishes were honoured in this remarkable way. The reference to the plunder by Sabean force is to the Roundheads who attacked and plundered the church as shown by the mute witness of the number of musket balls extracted from the south door. Weare was an enthusiastic Royalist whose property was sequestered in the Civil War.

Places of interest in the Neighbourhood
7. The Battle in the Pulpit (Abbotsbury)
8. The Ancient Stone Cross (Langton Herring)
10. The Altar Stone the Reformers missed (Corton Chapel, Portesham)
49. The Tranquil Ruined Chapel hidden in a coppice (Abbotsbury)

Food and Accommodation
'The Kings Arms' and the 'Half Moon Hotel' both serve good snacks. Accommodation, bed and breakfast at several houses in the village.

34 The Dole Table

Position. In the churchyard of Powerstock Church
Ordnance Map. Dorchester and Weymouth. Sheet 194 1.50000
Map Ref. 5170/9630
Access. From Dorchester take the A37 (Yeovil Road) as far as the
junction with the A356. Take the A356 here to Maiden Newton.
Continue on the A356 for about 4 miles when you will see Kingcombe
cross roads. Take road to Higher Kingcombe and directly on to
Powerstock (about 5 miles).

Note. In the churchyard east of the path and south of the main door is a
very rare survival, a 13th century Dole Table from which in pre-
reformation times charitable doles of bread were distributed to the poor.
It is still in good condition. Inside the church note the magnificent 12th
century Norman Chancel Arch.

Places of interest in the Neighbourhood
47. The Strange Story of the Posy Tree (Mapperton)

Food and Accommodation
Excellent beer and bar snacks available at the 'Three Horseshoes'.
Accommodation available at Crewkerne, 4 miles westward on the A356.

35 The Ice-House Where the ''Glorious Revolution'' of 1688 was Plotted

Position. In the grounds of Charborough House, Morden
Ordnance Map. Bere Regis. SY89/99 1.25000
Map Ref. 9260/9780
Access. Take the Dorchester road (A31) for about 4 miles, where you will see a high arch with a white stag on top, this is the entrance to Charborough House. The Grove Ice-House stands 30 yards north west of the house.

History. This humble building in the remote Dorset countryside played a large part in the history of England, for it was here in 1686 that a group of men met to plan the overthrow of James II and to replace him by the Dutch Prince of Orange, later William III. In the gable end is a modern marble inscription tablet, replacing a similar one of earlier date now in the picture gallery, which tells the whole story it reads:

''Under this roof, in the year MDCLXXXVI, a set of patriotic gentlemen of this neighbourhood concerted the great plan of the Glorious Revolution with the immortal King William; to whom we owe our deliverence from Popery and Slavery, and expulsion of the tyrant race of Stuarts; the restoration of our Liberty, the security of our property, and establishment of National Honour. Englishmen, remember this glorious area, and consider that your Liberties, procured by the vertues of your ancestors, must be maintained by yourselves.''

Thomas Erle Drax erected this stone, in the year MDCCLXXX. The archway opens to a porch or lobby with a semicircular vault faced with stucco; at the inner and is a nail-studded plank door with strap-hinges that opens a brick-lined passage leading to a circular ice-house. This last is some 12ft in diameter, brick-lined and with a domical roof with a central opening. The whole structure, behind the front, is earth covered.

Note. This very interesting site is not normally accessible to the public as it is in the grounds of a private house. Permission to view should be obtained from the Estate Office at Charborough Park, Wareham, Dorset. Alternatively the house and grounds are usually open once a year for a fête and in aid of charity, when it is possible to view it.

Charborough House, Morden, the north east front.

Places of interest in the Neighbourhood
11. The Ancient Astronomical Clock (Wimborne Minster)
14. The Man in the Wall (Wimborne Minster)
15. The Leper Hospital (Wimborne)
21. The Remarkable Roof (Bere Regis Church)
22. The Ancient Hour Glass (Bloxworth)
41. The Red Sign Post (Anderson)

Food and Accommodation
Ample at Wimborne or Dorchester.

36 Where the King Escaped and the History of England was Changed

Position. Bridport
Ordnance Map. Bridport. SY49 1.25000
Map Ref. 4800/9330
Access. Just as you enter Bridport from Dorchester where there is a sign "Bridport" there is a little lane on the right hand side, "Lee Lane", and on the wall is a stone monument.

Note. The monument has the following inscription "King Charles II escaped capture through this lane Sept XXIII. MDCLI. When midst your fiercest foes on everyside for your escape God did a lane provide". Behind the simple statement lies the romantic story of the King's escape after the defeat at the Battle of Worcester. Charles had made his way to Bristol then turned eastwards trying to escape by sea from Charmouth. This failed and he now made his way to Bridport. Unknown to Charles the alarm had been raised at Charmouth and as Charles was leaving Bridport on the morning of Sept 23rd 1651 at the eastern end Capt. Macey with a troop of Roundhead soldiers entered the western end. At Lee Lane Charles and his companions decided on the spur of the moment to make for Trent where there was a priest hole in the Manor House to provide a safe refuge. Macey could hardly have missed them by more than five minutes as he thundered past the opening of this insignificant track on his way to Dorchester. Thus the king escaped and nine years later returned from France to be crowned King. If Charles had been captured he would undoubtedly have been executed, changing the whole history of England.

Places of interest in the Neighbourhood
47. The Posy Tree and its Strange Story (Mapperton)

Food and Accommodation
Ample available at Bridport.

KING CHARLES II
ESCAPED CAPTURE THROUGH THIS LANE
SEP. XXIII. MDCLI.
WHEN MIDST YOUR FIERCEST FOES ON EVERY SIDE
FOR YOUR ESCAPE GOD DID A LANE PROVIDE.
(THOMAS FULLERS WORTHIES)
ERECTED SEP. XXIII MDCCCCI.
A.M.D.

37 The Agglestone

Position. On heath near Studland

Ordnance Map. Purbeck SY 87/97SZ07 1.25000

Map Ref. 0240/8290

Access. From Corfe Castle take the road to Studland (B3351) for about four miles. At this point you will see Golf Club and car park on left hand side. Continue on round the bend in the road where you will find parking space with a sign post "Footpath to Agglestone". Follow path and shortly afterwards you will see on right hand side a further sign post "To the Agglestone". Continue across heath on this path until you reach the Agglestone itself.

Note. This huge rock, in a superb setting overlooking the sea and Poole Harbour, is made of ferruginous Sandstone and is 18ft. high, 80ft. in circumference and weighs about 400 tons. The Agglestone is all that is left of a thick layer of sandstone which once covered the heath and which was eroded by time and the elements. The views out to sea and over Poole Harbour on a fine day are magnificent.

Places of interest in the Neighbourhood

60. The Splendid Effigy that Salisbury Cathedral did not want (Wareham)

Food and Accommodation

Ample available in Studland and Swanage.

38 The Column Which Solved the meaning of Egyptian Hieroglyphs

Position. Kingston Lacy House, near Wimborne
Ordnance Map. Tarrant ST90. 1.25000
Map Ref. 9780/0120
Access. Take the B3082 from Wimborne for about two miles when you will see Kingston Lacy House on your left hand side. The house is a National Trust property and opening times should be checked.

Note. This stone column is called the Philae Needle and is an ancient Egyptian obelisk. It is on the lawn south of Kingston Lacy House (now

owned by the National Trust). Before 1822 Egyptian hieroglyphs were thought to be symbols and nobody could read them. In 1822, however, Jean Francis Champollion, using the Rosetta stone and the Philae Needle, was able to decipher the hieroglyphics, proving that they were letters. The inscription around the base tells the full story. ''William John Banks Esq M.P. eldest son of Henry Banks Esq M.P. caused this obelisk and the pedestal from which it had fallen to be removed under the direction of G. Belzoni in 1819 from the island of Philae beyond the first cateract and brought this platform - the stepped base from the nuns of Hierassycaminon in Nubia. The granite used in the preparation of this monument was brought from the remains of Lepis Magna in Africa and was given for that purpose by His Majesty King George IV.'' The inscriptions on this obelisk and pedestal record their dedications to King Ptolemy Euergetes II and his two queens who authorised the priest of Isis on the isle of Philae to erect them about 150 B.C. as a perpetual memorial of exemption from taxation. This spot was chosen and the first stone of the foundation laid by Arthur, Duke of Wellington, August 17, 1827.

Places of interest in the Neighbourhood
 1. The Medieval Amplifiers (Tarrant Rushton)
11. The Astronomical Clock (Wimborne Minster)
14. The Man in the Wall (Wimborne Minster)
15. The Leper Hospital (Wimborne)

Food and Accommodation
There are many restaurants and tea rooms in Wimborne whilst accommodation may be obtained at the Kings Head Hotel in the Square.

39 The Unique Post Box

Position. Barnes Cross, Holwell
Ordnance Map. Sherborne. ST61 1.25000
Map Ref. 6920/1160
Access. From Bishops Caundle turn left down Milburn Lane. At the end of Milburn lane turn left and shortly afterwards you will see a pair of stone cottages in front of which is the post box.

Note. This pillar box is the oldest pillar box still in use in Great Britain. It was made by John N. Butt and company of Gloucester between 1853 and 1856. Apart from being made of metal and painted red it is very different from the sort of post box we use today. It is octagonal instead of circular with the words ''Post Office Letterbox'' cast at the top, above Queen Victoria's cipher and the maker's name. The box is about five feet high and each angle of the eight sides is fluted, which gives it a distinctive appearance.

The slot for the letters is very small (less then 1 inch wide by 5½ inches deep) and is vertical instead of horizontal. A swinging flap, on the inside of the hole, keeps out the rain.

Places of interest in the Neighbourhood
32. The Strange Case of the Modest Lady of Lydlinch (Lydlinch)

Food and Accommodation
Ample at Sherborne.

40 The Saxon Shrine

Position. In the Church of St Wite, Whitchurch Canonicorum
Ordnance Map. Axminster. SY29/39 1.25000
Map Ref. 3970/9550
Access. From Chideock take the A35 westwards for about 1½ miles.
Turn right at signpost to Whitchurch Canonicorum. The church is in the
centre of the village.

Note. This beautiful church has several very rare things, the rarest being
the Shrine to a Saxon Saint, St Wite or Candida. The Shrine is probably
the only pre-reformation shrine to have survived. It is still intact and
consists of two parts; a 13th century base brought from some other place,
and rebuilt in its present position to bear the upper part, which is of older
date. The three oval openings beneath on the tomb are a common feature
of such monuments. In these openings handkerchiefs and other small
articles were placed in the belief that they would become possessed of
healing virtues and could then be used to help the sick. The coffin was
opened by the Rev. Sir William Palmer and was said to contain a small
stone box in which were a few bones, but no documentary evidence
remains of his act, nor any record of what he found there. On the top
stands a small stone cross much decayed, which formed the finial of the
east gable of the chancel. It was placed here for its preservation by the
Rev. J. R. W. Stafford, a former vicar, in 1890. A second opportunity
for examining the contents of the tomb presented itself, for in March
1900, an ominous fissure appeared in the north wall, and it was necessary
to underpin the walls, which was done by the Vicar. The movement of
the soil and consequent settlement dislocated the old shrine, re-opening
an ancient fracture in the stone coffin to such an extent that it became
necessary to reset the broken end. It was during the execution of this
work that the re-discovery of the relics was made. The broken end of the
coffin having been withdrawn, there was seen the end of a leaden casket
eight inches square.

This proved to be the square end of an oblong, ancient, leaden
reliquary of 2ft. 5ins. It was badly damaged, having been ripped open
from end to end. The incrustation of oxide on the torn edges seemed to
show that the damage was not recent, apparently it had been done
centuries before. In the reliquary were a number of large bones, a good
deal decayed, presumably those of a small woman. These were not
disturbed in their resting place, but one of the bones which lay upper-

most, was measured and found to be 13⅞ ins long. The large fragments found on the floor of the coffin were placed with the bones in the reliquary and all the smaller fragments and dust reverently collected into a small metal box and placed within the coffin. One side of the reliquary was complete and undamaged and on it was found cast in raised letters the following inscription:-

✠hICREQESCT·RELIQE · SCE·WITE

(Here lie the remains of Saint Wita.)

The whole of the relics were carefully replaced in the stone coffin, the broken end being securely cemented in place.

The other items of interest are the Norman Doorway and the Sanctus Bell on the roof which in pre-reformation times was rung at the elevation of the host at Mass to tell the labourers in the fields.

Another point of interest is that Sir George Somers the discoverer of Bermuda is buried here but only a modern brass recalls the fact.

Food and Accommodation
Ample at Chideock.

41 The Red Sign Post

Position. On the A31 Wimborne to Dorchester road about 5 miles from Wimborne
Ordnance Map. Bere Regis. SY8999 1.25000
Map Ref. 8840/9710

Note. This sign post has been a source of much speculation as to its origin, and even the County Authorities who paint it red at regular intervals did not know why they did so until recently. The legends of

murder and gibbets can be discounted, but the real reason for the colour of the sign post is as strange as any legend. If one turns at the Red Sign Post down the lane to Bloxworth, after 100 yards you will see a farm called Botany Bay Farm on your right hand side. In it is a half-destroyed barn built like a prison with very narrow slits for windows. This barn was built in the late 18th century and was used to house prisoners condemned at Dorchester to transportation for life to Australia. The condemned prisoners had to walk from Dorchester to Portsmouth for embarkation and Botany Bay Farm was used for the first night's stop, it being 14 miles from the prison. In those days a vast majority of people were illiterate, including the guards, and the post painted red as a sign to them to turn off with their prisoners for lodging in the barn. The barn, which was partly destroyed in 1935, had at one time a large pole in the centre, rising to the roof, to which the prisoners were attached by chains for the night.

Places of interest in the Neighbourhood
  3. The Church that Hardy saved (Winterborne Tomson)
22. The Ancient Hour Glass (Bloxworth)

Food and Accommodation
On the main road from Wimborne to Dorchester there are many villages which offer refreshment of all kinds. Accommodation, ample at Dorchester and Wimborne.

42 The Oldest Houses in Britain

Position. Eggardon. (5 miles N.E. Bridport. 11 miles N.W. Dorchester)
Ordnance Map. Maiden Newton. SY59 1.25000
Map Ref. 5420/9460
Access. From Bridport and places west take the Bridport-Dorchester road (A35) for four miles east of Bridport. On the left hand side there is a turning to Askerswell. Take this road and go right through the village. At T junction take road to right. This will take you directly to Eggardon Hill which is clearly visible (2 miles). Coming from Dorchester take the main Bridport road for 3 miles and then carry on the old Roman road marked to Compton Valence. Follow this Roman road until you reach, (after a further 6 miles) a road running alongside Eggardon. Access from where you leave your car is simple and level.

Note. The centre of the fort is 20 acres in extent and in Stone Age times was quite heavily populated. There are no less than 123 depressions which, when excavated, have been found to be the homes of Stone Age man. They were 10ft. in diameter and the earth was dug to a depth of 6ft. 8in., with a 2ft. base layer of flints to act as drainage. The floor was then covered with heather and furze. The rim of the pits was 2ft. of excavated earth and on top of this poles or branches were placed tent-wise at 45 degrees to meet in the centre thus making a snug refuge on a winter's night from the great gales whistling overhead. Anyone who has ever spent an hour on a windy day on Eggardon Hill will realise what a relief it must have been to get in these pit-dwellings - cold, damp and uncomfortable as they must have been. Yet these primitive people, whose lives were short and brutish, racked with arthritis, built their homes solely with antler-pick and reed basket and their walls have outlasted many a great palace built of stone and marble.

Places of interest in the Neighbourhood
34. The Dole Table (Powerstock)
47. The Strange Story of the Posy Tree (Mapperton)

Food and Accommodation
Ample accommodation at Bridport. Refreshments available at the 'Three Horseshoes' at Powerstock where excellent bar meals are served.

43 The Gibbet that became a Sun Dial

Position. West Parley Churchyard
Ordnance Map. Bournemouth West. SZ09 1.25000
Map Ref. 0870/9680
Access. From Wimborne take the by-pass eastwards as far as Longham, here turn left and almost immediately right towards Christchurch. After about a mile you reach Parley crossroads. Cross straight over and take first turning on right marked Church Lane. Follow road down as far as church.

Note. Entering the churchyard you will see on the right hand side a Sun Dial mounted on a very old wooden post. Local tradition will tell you that the post was the post of a gibbet, which once stood on Parley Common (there is no reason to doubt this since the gibbet was known to exist).

Apparently the last time the gibbet was used was in 1803 when Jonathan Harben and John Gubby were executed at Winchester for murder and then subsequently strung up on a gibbet on Parley Common as a warning to others. The owner of the land was eventually disgusted by the vast numbers of sightseers who came to see those poor wretches and he had the gibbet cut down and handed over part of the post to the Rector of West Parley who had it set up in the churchyard as the base for the Sun Dial we see today.

Places of interest in the Neighbourhood
16. The Mystery of the Jesuit Tombs (Hampreston Church)
32. The Strange Case of the Modest Lady of Lydlinch (West Parley)
55. The Empty Tomb and the Tragic Countess (Christchurch)

Food and Accommodation
Ample available at Christchurch, and Wimborne.

44 The Rails from the Royal Tomb in Westminster Abbey

Position. Piddletrenthide School
Ordnance Map. Puddletown. SY79 1.25000
Map Ref. 7070/9960
Access. From Puddletown take the B3142 to Piddlehinton then the B3143 which leads directly to Piddletrenthide. The school, where the rails act as gates, is in the centre of the village.

Note. These gates certainly came from Westminster Abbey and are those which surrounded the tomb of Mary, Queen of Scots, although some claim that they came from the tomb of Margaret, Countess of Richmond. The gates came to Piddletrenthide because a certain Mr Bridge, a wealthy silversmith to the Court of George III and IV who lived at the Manor House, bought them in 1826 for £110 when restoration was being done to Westminster Abbey. The gates were subsequently hung at the Manor House until 1911, when the house was sold. The greater part of the railings were returned to Westminster Abbey, this pair of gates was missed and subsequently installed in position outside the village school. Certainly they are very historic, for they date back to the reign of James I who built the tomb for his martyred mother in Westminster Abbey and had these gates installed around it.

Places of interest in the Neighbourhood
45. The Earliest use of Arabic letters in any Church in England (Piddletrenthide Church)

Food and Accommodation
Available at Piddletrenthide and Puddletown.

45 The Earliest use of Arabic Numerals in any Church in England

Position. Piddletrenthide Church
Ordnance Map. Dorchester and Weymouth. Sheet 194 1.50000
Map Ref. 7010/0080
Access. From Puddletown take the B3142 to Piddlehinton, then the B3143 which leads directly to Piddletrenthide.

Note. Over the west door of the tower is written in Latin the following phrases:-

> Est pydeltrenth villa in dorsedie comitatu Nascitur in illa quam rexit Vicariatu 1487.

> (It is in Piddletrenthide, a town in Dorset (where) he was born (and) where he is Vicar, 1487).

It is certainly most remarkable that in such a remote village Arabic numerals were used when Roman numerals continued for at least another century everywhere else.

Places of interest in the Neighbourhood
44. The Rails from the Royal Tomb in Westminster Abbey (Piddletrenthide)

Food and Accommodation
Bar meals and refreshments may be obtained at the 'Poachers Inn', and Puddletown.

46 The Mystery of the Lone Pillar at Cross and Hand

Position. On the road from Minterne Magna to Evershot
Ordnance Map. Cerne Abbas. ST60 1.25000
Map Ref. 6302/0380
Access. Go to Minterne Magna (halfway between Dorchester and
Sherborne, A352). At Minterne Magna running westwards is a small
upland road to Evershot and the Lone Pillar is on the right hand side of
the road about 1½ miles from Minterne Magna and about 100 yards past
the crossroads at Cross and Hand.

Note. This stone pillar is about 4ft. high and 1 ft. wide and stands in total isolation. It is mentioned by Hardy in *Tess of the D'Urbervilles*: "'Tis a thing of ill-omen, Miss. It was put up in wild times by the relations of a malefactor who was tortured there by nailing his hands to a post and afterwards hung. The bones lie underneath. They say he sold his soul to the devil, and that he walks at times". Hardy also refers to it in his poem 'The Lost Pyx', evoking a wild stormy night and a priest from nearby Cerne Abbey being called out to shrive a dying man in this remote upland cottage. On arrival, the priest discovers that he has dropped the sacrament along the way. He retraces his steps, miraculously finding it being protected by a circle of wild animals and lit by a ray of light. Later, the priest raises the stone - "to mark where shone that midnight miracle."

Despite the legends the general opinion of most authorities is that it is a Roman pillar, probably from a temple in the area, and was put in its present site to mark a boundary since it has a Government bench mark chiselled into its south face. The area is wild and lonely, and it is not surprising that Hardy should use it as the source for a poem. The stone is grey, but is yellow with lichen.

Places of interest in the Neighbourhood
12. The Madonna that escaped the fury of the Reformation (Cerne Abbas)
19. The Well of St Augustin (Cerne Abbas)

Food and Accommodation
These are available at Cerne Abbas.

47 The Strange Story of the Posy Tree

Position. Posy Tree: at Mapperton near Beaminster. Mass grave. South
Warren Hill, Melplash.
Ordnance Map. Posy Tree. Dorchester & Weymouth Sheet 194 1.50000
Mass Grave. Bridport. Sheet SY49 1.25000
Map Ref. Posy Tree. 4980/9960 Mass Grave. 4830/9910
Access to Posy Tree. From Dorchester take the road to Yeovil (A37) and
turn off to Maiden Newton (A356) after a few miles. Carry on along the
A356 for some miles until you see signpost to Beaminster (B3163) take
this road and after 2½ miles there is a road on left-hand-side leading to

Mapperton. Carry on after passing the Manor House until you see a sycamore tree, with the following inscription on it, "The Posy Tree". In Sept 1666 the Great Plague reached its peak and it was here Mapperton survivors gathered wild herbs and flowers to ward off the plague as the bodies of the dead were taken up this lane for burial in a common grave.

Note. This notice is wrong in almost every detail. The plague which killed some 80 inhabitants took place in 1582 and the story of the tree is quite different. For years the dead of Mapperton had been buried in Netherbury churchyard, because the soil at Mapperton was unsuitable, and the way from the tree to Netherbury is still called "Dead Man's Lane". On the occasion however, of the plague, the inhabitants of Netherbury gathered at the tree armed with staves and refused to allow the corpses of the Mapperton dead to be buried in the village. After a fight, the inhabitants of Mapperton had to retreat to South Warren Hill, where, on the summit, they buried their dead in a mass grave and over it they planted a copse of conifers so that the ground would not be disturbed for many years.

Access to Mass Grave. Return to main road and continue on to Beaminster. Then take the road to Bridport and after 1½ miles on your left, you will see a sign post; "Bridleway to Mapperton 1¾ miles". Park your car here and walk to summit of hill, where you will see the plantation of conifers and the mass grave.

Note. The view from here is truly magnificent. On a tree near the entrance from the road is a memorial to Lt. Moorhouse who in 1915 became the first member of the Royal Flying Corps to be awarded the V.C.

Places of interest in the Neighbourhood
53. The Beautiful Tower (Beaminster)

Food and Accommodation
Excellent at several Hotels and Inns in Beaminster.

48 The Glorious Avenue of Trees

Position. About 4 miles north of Wimborne on the B3082 to Blandford.
Ordnance Map. Blandford Forum ST80/90 1.25000 Pathfinder Series
Map Ref. 9730/0210
Access. Take the B3082 from Wimborne and after about 4 miles you will
see the great avenue of trees before you.

Note. There are three hundred and sixty-five beeches on either side over
a distance of 2.2 miles. In spring, summer and autumn the trees make a
canopy of leaves unsurpassed in beauty by any avenue in England.
These trees were planted in 1835, according to legend by one now
forgotten woodman on the Kingston Lacy Estate, and make what must
surely be one of the finest avenues in Europe.

Places of interest in the Neighbourhood
   1. The Medieval Amplifiers (Tarrant Rushton Church)
  11. The Ancient Astronomical Clock (Wimborne Minster)
  14. The Man in the Wall (Wimborne Minster)
  15. The Leper Hospital (Wimborne)
  38. The Column which solves the Meaning of Egyptian Hieroglyphs
      (Kingston Lacy House)

Food and Accommodation
Ample selection at Wimborne, and Blandford.

49 The Ruined Chapel Hidden in a Coppice

Position. In a coppice north west of Abbotsbury Castle
Ordnance Map. Abbotsbury Sheet SY58 1.25000
Map Ref. 5570/8790
Access. Starting from Abbotsbury, take the B3157 westwards for 1½ miles to the top of Abbotsbury hill. Here you will see a sign post on the right to Ashley Chase. Follow this for ½ mile when you will see the entrance leading to Ashley Chase marked ''Private''. Just before this, you will see a track veering northwest on your left. Park your car here and follow this track for about 1 mile, where at the foot of a hill you will see a coppice on the right hand side with a stile leading into it. Go over the stile and into the coppice where a footpath, just visible, will lead you directly to the ruined Chapel.

Note. These remains of a 13th century Cistercian cell are beautifully sited overlooking a small ravine with a stream flowing at the bottom. Inside the Chapel are the tombs of David and Olga Milne-Watson, who built Ashley Chase House, and the tomb of a friend. At the other end of the roofless Chapel is a small altar built of stones from the ruins on which stands a crucifix with the figure of Christ wearing a crown. A plaque on the Chapel wall asks for prayers for the repose of the souls of David and Olga Milne-Watson.

Places of interest in the Neighbourhood
  7. The Battle in the Pulpit (Abbotsbury)

Food and Accommodation
At the 'Ilchester Arms', and 'The Swan' in Abbotsbury, one can purchase drinks, good bar meals and receive a cheerful welcome.

50 The Man who opened Tibet to the West

Position. Lytchett Minster churchyard
Ordnance Map. Bere Regis Sheet SY 89/99 1.25000
Map Ref. 9610/9310

Note. In the Churchyard directly behind the Church is the grave of the explorer Sir Francis Younghusband, who, in 1902, led an expedition through the Himalayas into the unknown kingdom of Tibet. As well as opening up the country to Western influence and trade by the signing of a treaty with the Dalai Lama, he was the enthusiastic spirit behind the first three expeditions to Everest. A deeply religious man, he founded in 1936 the World Council of Churches. The headstone is remarkable for the carving of the great palace of the Dalai Lama in Lhasa. The church, which was re-built in 1903, contains little of interest.

Places of interest in the Neighbourhood
  1. The Ancient Astronomical Clock (Wimborne Minster)
14. The Man in the Wall (Wimborne Minster)
15. The Leper Hospital (Wimborne)
51. The Knight who murdered his King "most vilely"
     (Lytchett Matravers)

Food and Accommodation
''The St Peter's Finger'', opposite the church serves good bar meals and drinks. Accommodation available at Wimborne, or Poole.

51 The Knight who Murdered his King "Most Vilely"

Position. Lytchett Matravers Church
Ordnance Map. Bere Regis Sheet SY 89/99 1.25000
Map Ref. 9350/9620
Access. The church lies alone in the fields well outside the village. This is due to the wiping out of the old village during the Black Death. The new village was built well away from the plague area. From the village follow the High Street along the B3075 northward for about half a mile, where at the bottom of the hill is a turning to the left with a cattle grid. The Church is up this lane.

Note. Standing in this beautiful little Church alone in the fields it is difficult to realise that here in a humble grave beneath the floor lies one who in his day was one of the most powerful men in England, and who murdered his King, Edward II, in a most horrible way. Sir John Maltravers and Sir Thomas de Berkley were appointed to guard Edward II, imprisoned at Berkeley Castle and during the absence of Sir Thomas, as Highden tells us "Edward was most ignominiously slain with a red hot spit thrust into the anus". It is believed that a spit was employed so as to show no signs of external injury. On the accession of Edward III Sir John fled to Flanders but was later pardoned and returned to his estates in Dorset. He is said to be buried in full armour in a tomb beneath the floor in the North Aisle. He died here in 1365 and his epitaph claimed he was a good knight in war and peace.

Do not miss the small but very beautiful brass of Thomas Pethryn on the sanctuary wall. This is the only surviving example of a shroud brass in Dorset.

Places of interest in the Neighbourhood
  1. The Ancient Astronomical Clock (Wimborne Minster)
  14. The Man in the Wall (Wimborne Minster)
  15. The Leper Hospital (Wimborne)
  50. The Man who Opened Tibet to the West (Lytchett Minster)

Food and Accommodation
The Chequers Inn at Lytchett Matravers does very good bar meals, accommodation available at Wimborne, or Poole.

52 The Woman Who Did What She Could

Position. Hampreston Church
Ordnance Map. Bournemouth Sheet 179 1.50000
Map Ref. 0550/9870
Access. From Wimborne take the by-pass to Ringwood. At the end of the by-pass is a road to Longham. Take this for about 1 mile when on the right hand side is a turning to Hampreston.

Note. Amongst the thousand of epitaphs in Churches and churchyards in Dorset there are many moving ones that repay study, but high on the wall of the Chancel in Hampreston church is one that brings a smile to the lips and warms the heart. It reads as follows:-

> Sacred to the Memory of
> Edward Greathed
> of Uddens House, County of Dorset
> Born Jan 1st 1777
> Died Dec 1st 1840
> And of Mary Elizabeth, his wife
> only daughter of
> Sir Richard Glyn. Bart
> who bore him five sons and four daughters
> Born May 18th 1786
> Died Jan 17th 1864
> "She did what she could"

Since Mary Elizabeth died long after her husband it is puzzling to know who wrote the strange but moving tribute. Did Elizabeth herself write it with tongue in cheek? Or did one of her numerous children give her a genuine tribute?

Strangely enough within two generations this large family had died out and another family was established at Uddens House.

Places of interest in the Neighbourhood
16. The Mystery of the Jesuit Tombs (Hampreston Church)

Food and Accommodation
Ample available at Wimborne.

[88]

53 The Beautiful Tower

Position. Beaminster
Ordnance Map. Taunton and Lyme Regis. Sheet 193 1.50000
Map Ref. 4800/0130
Access. The Parish Church of St Mary is just off the town square via Church Lane.

Note. The tower of St Mary's was built just before the Reformation in 1503. Because, by some strange chance, it escaped the usual vandalism that accompanied the Reformation, it still possesses some of the finest pre-Reformation carvings to be seen anywhere. On the lower part, the roof corbels are carved with the symbols of the Evangelists, eagle, phoenix, fox and snake, fox and goose, angel and grotesque beasts. Higher is a canopied niche containing the image of the Virgin and Child flanked by the figures of St James and St George. Above is a carved Crucifix with the Virgin and St John and above this panel are three pinnacles standing on angel corbels and between them two small panels under canopies carved with a Resurrection and an Ascension. Flanking the pinnacles are two secular figures, one is dressed as a pilgrim to Compostella complete with cockle shell badge in his hat, the other is dressed as a fuller with his implement; at this level are pinnacles set against the buttresses standing on carved beasts. It is said that rebels supporting Monmouth's Rebellion were hanged from the tower.

Places of interest in the Neighbourhood
The Church itself is well worth a visit. Do not miss the memorial to Betty Pavy in the churchyard which reads as follows:-

> Sacred to ye remains of ye unfortunate Betty Daughter to William and Ann Pavy aged 23 who fell a sacrifice in ye Dreadful Conflagration which happened in this town on Saturday March ye 31st 1781

42. The Oldest Houses in Britain (Eggardon Hill)
47. The Strange Story of the Posy Tree (Mapperton)

Food and Accommodation
Excellent food and accommodation available in Beaminster.

54 Where the Boy King sat under the Great Oak and touched for the King's Evil

Position. Woodlands
Ordnance Map. Bournemouth Sheet 179 1.50000
Map Ref. 0500/1000
Access. Starting from the Square at Wimborne take the road to Cranborne (B3078) for 8.4 miles when you will see a signpost to

Ringwood. Turn right here and follow the road for 1 mile. Here is a signpost on the right-hand-side to "Woodlands and Horton". Stop car here as immediately opposite is an oak of great age; it is so old that the inside is hollow. At the foot of the tree is a plaque which reads "According to tradition King Edward VI sat beneath this tree and touched for the King's Evil".

Note. Scrofula, or the King's Evil (scurvy and similar skin ailments), could be supposedly cured if anyone suffering from it was touched by a reigning monarch. Edward VI, the 'boy King', was probably more in need of help than most of his supplicants, for in 1553, at the age of sixteen, he died of tuberculosis.

Places of interest in the Neighbourhood
 1. The Medieval Amplifiers (Tarrant Rushton Church)
 5. The Folly that Humphrey Sturt Built (Horton)
58. The Philosphers Tower (Monkton up Wimborne)
75. The Sacred Circle (Knowlton)

Food and Accommodation
'The King's Head' at Wimborne and the 'Fleur de Lys' at Cranborne, both provide good food and accommodation.

55 The Empty Tomb and the Tragic Countess

Position. Christchurch Priory
Ordnance Map. Bournemouth East Sheet SZ 19 1.25000
Map Ref. 1600/9250

Note. On the north side of the chancel in Christchurch Priory is a very beautiful Chantry Chapel built by Margaret, Countess of Salisbury, for her own last resting place.

This tragic lady was the daughter of the Duke of Clarence, brother to Edward IV. Her father was drowned in a butt of Malmsey wine on her brother's orders and her brother and eldest son were executed for high treason. Another son, Cardinal Pole, wrote a book attacking Henry VIII for claiming to be head of the Church in England. Henry VIII reacted with characteristic rage. The Countess of Salisbury, who was over 70, was imprisoned for two years and then ordered to be beheaded. She refused to put her head on the block and it was hacked from her body whilst standing. Henry VIII pursued his vengeance even after her death by not allowing her to be buried in this beautiful tomb, but in the chapel reserved for traitors in the Tower of London, St Peter's Chapel. She was the last of the great Plantagenets who had ruled over England for so long, and was finally beatified by Pope Leo XIII in 1886.

Whilst in the Priory, which has much to see, do not miss the memorial of the Countess Fitzharris, of Heron Court, a young mother who died in 1815, shown sitting with a baby in her arms whilst two boys in long trousers look into her face as she read to them. The graceful composition is very moving and is one of Flaxman's finest pieces.

Places of interest in the Neighbourhood
32. The Strange case of the Modest Lady of Lydlinch (West Parley)
43. The Gibbet that became a Sun Dial (West Parley)

Food and Accommodation
Ample in Christchurch and Bournemouth.

56 The Hiding Place which Saved the Life of Charles II

Position. Trent Manor House, Trent
Ordnance Map. Yeovil & Frome Sheet 183 1.50000
Map Ref. 5910/1850
Access. Trent lies 3 miles N.W. of Sherborne, and can be reached by either going north out of Sherborne on the B1438 for Marston Magna or turning north off the A30 approximately mid-way between Yeovil and Sherborne on the road marked Over Compton and Trent.

Note. After the disastrous Battle of Worcester in June 1651 Charles II fled to the West Country hoping to escape to France from one of the Dorset ports. During his hazardous journey he found shelter for nineteen days at Trent Manor House, the home of Colonel Francis Wyndham who had married Anne Gerard, a member of a noted Catholic family and owners of the Manor House for generations. The house was considered especially suitable as it had a double hiding hole built to conceal hunted priests during penal times. The hide was at one end of the room in which the King lay concealed and was available to him if soldiers had come to search the house. Charles left Trent for Heale House, near Salisbury, finally sailing for France from what is now Brighton.

The Manor House is in private hands and not normally open to inspection. It is however occasionally opened during the summer for garden fêtes and of course one can always apply to the owner for permission to see the hide.

Places of interest in the Neighbourhood
32. The Strange Case of the Modest Lady of Lydlinch (Lydlinch)

Food and Accommodation
Freely available in Sherborne.

Hiding Place.   Interior.

57 The Cottage Orné

Position. On the road to Cranborne from Wimborne (B3078)
Ordnance Map. Bournemouth Sheet 179 1.50000
Map Ref. 0060/0680
Access. From Wimborne take the B3078 road to Cranborne for 2½ miles. On the right hand side just before entering the village of Stanbridge you will see the beautiful and unique cottage, known as the Cottage Orné.

Note. This early 19th century cottage was formerly a lodge at the gate way to Gaunts House. It is of one storey with an attic and has brick walls and a thatch roof.

Places of interest in the Neighbourhood
  5. The Folly that Humphrey Sturt Built (Horton)
11. The Ancient Astronomical Clock (Wimborne Minster)
14. The Man in the Wall (Wimborne Minster)
15. The Leper Hospital (Wimborne)
58. The Philosopher's Tower (off Cranborne/Wimborne road)
75. The Sacred Circle (Knowlton)

Food and Accommodation
Plenty available in Wimborne, and 'The Fleur de Lys' at Cranborne.

58 The Philosopher's Tower

Position. On the road to Cranborne from Wimborne (B3078)
Ordnance Map. Cranborne Sheet SU01 1.25000
Map Ref. 0450/1090
Access. From Wimborne take the B3078 to Cranborne for 8½ miles. At

8½ miles there is a sign post to Woodlands; carry on past this for 200 yards when you will see a gate into a field on the right hand side. The field goes up a slight slope and after 100 yards the tower comes into view.

Note. This square two-storey tower or Gazebo, has rounded brick walls and a domical roof covered with tiles and lead. It was built c.1700 as a place of contemplation for the 3rd Earl of Shaftesbury, known as the Philosopher Earl. Presumably he wished to copy the example of the great French philosopher Montaigne who first set the fashion for philosophers to live in a tower. The east side has a plain square-headed doorway and a large sashed window in the upper storey. The north and west sides have similar windows; the west side also has an oval ground floor window and a plain door giving access to a small cellar. The south side bears a stone cartouche of the arms of the 2nd Earl.

Places of interest in the Neighbourhood
   5. The Tower that Humphrey Sturt Built (Horton)
  17. The place where the would-be King was captured   (Woodlands)
  54. Where the boy King sat under the Great Oak and touched for the King's Evil (Woodlands)
  57. The Cottage Orné (Stanbridge)
  75. The Sacred Circle (Knowlton)

Food and Accommodation
At the 'Fleur de Lys', Cranborne.

59 The Tragic Story of Lady Smith and her Lost Children

Position. Sydling St Nicholas Church
Ordnance Map. Dorchester & Weymouth Sheet 194 1.50000
Map Ref. 6300/9940
Access. From Dorchester take the A37 to Yeovil road, for about 5 miles, when on the right hand side you will see an archway with a signpost to Sydling St Nicholas 3½ miles. Carry on as far as the village, where you will see the church standing alongside the Manor House.

Notes. On the north wall of the church there is an eighteenth century memorial tablet which tells a very tragic story. It is a memorial to the four sons and five daughters of Sir John and Lady Smith, who died so young in infancy that there was no time to christen them, and they are simply recorded as the infant children.

Places of interest in the Neighbourhood
30. The Room where Judge Jefferies held his Bloody Assize (Dorchester)
61. The Hangman's Cottage (Dorchester)

Food and Accommodation
Ample available in Dorchester

60 The Splendid Effigy that Salisbury Cathedral did not want

Position. In the little Saxon church of St Martin, at Wareham
Ordnance Map. Wareham Sheet SY88/98 1.25000
Map Ref. 9230/8770
Access. As you enter Wareham from the Poole or Blandford Roads,
there is a slight rise. At the top of the rise on the left hand side is a small
church, the church of St Martin.

Note. Inside the very tiny but beautiful Saxon Church, there is to be seen
a large reclining effigy of Lawrence of Arabia, dressed in full Arabic
costume. It is a magnificent piece of carving by one of our greatest
modern sculptors, Eric Kennington. Owing to its size it is however
entirely out of place in such a tiny church. The effigy was originally
designed to be placed in Salisbury Cathedral but the then Dean refused at
the last moment to accept it. The rector of Wareham was finally
persuaded to allow the effigy to be placed in the church of St Martin,
presumably because Lawrence of Arabia had many local connections. It
is however, totally out of place in its present position and is to be hoped
that someday a more suitable setting may be found for it. Do not miss the
pre-Reformation murals on the Chancel wall, which have recently been
uncovered.

Places of interest in the Neighbourhood
  4. The Creech Folly (West Creech Hill)
18. The Grave of a Hero (Moreton)
20. The Kimmeridge Folly (Kimmeridge)
37. The Agglestone (Studland)

Food and Accommodation
Ample in Wareham.

61 The Hangman's Cottage

Position. Dorchester
Ordnance Map. Dorchester & Weymouth Sheet 194 1.50000
Map Ref. 6960/9070
Access. Halfway up High East Street in Dorchester, on the right hand
side coming from Poole, is a Clock Tower at the turning into North
Square. Go through North Square and follow the road called Friary Hill,
which is alongside the prison. At the foot of the hill you will come to a
small stream with a foot bridge, pass over the foot bridge and turn left,
walk along the stream for about ½ mile, when you come to another foot
bridge turn left and almost immediately in front of you is the very pretty,
thatched Hangman's Cottage.

Note. In the 17th, 18th, and early 19th centuries hangings were almost a
weekly event in Dorchester and it was necessary for there to be a resident
hangman. This cottage is just below the prison and only a few minutes
walk to the scene of execution. Thomas Hardy refers to this cottage in

his famous short story *The Withered Arm*. It reads as follows: "At this date, and for several years after, there was a hangman to almost every jail. Gertrude found, on inquiry, that the Casterbridge official dwelt in a lonely cottage by a deep slow river flowing under the cliff on which the prison buildings were situate. Having changed her dress and before she had eaten or drunk - for she could not take her ease till she had ascertained some particulars - Gertrude pursued her way by a path along the waterside to the cottage indicated. Passing thus the out-skirts of the jail, she discerned on the level roof over the gateway three rectangular lines against the sky, where the specks had been moving in her distant view; she recognised what the erection was, and passed quickly on. Another hundred yards brought her to the executioner's house, which a boy pointed out. It stood close to the same stream and was hard by a weir, the waters of which emitted a steady roar.''

Places of interest in the Neighbourhood
  2. The Norman Tympanum and the Roman Tombstone
       (Fordington Church)
30. The Room where Judge Jefferies held his Bloody Assize
       (Dorchester)
31. The Flying Angel (Winterbourne Steepleton)

Food and Accommodation
Ample available in Dorchester.

62 The Chained Library

Position. Wimborne Minster
Ordnance Map. Bournemouth West Sheet SZ09 1.25000
Map Ref. 0090/9980

Note. This rare example of a Chained Library is open Monday to Friday
10.30 a.m. - 1.00 p.m. and 2.00 p.m. - 4.00 p.m.; there is a small
admission fee.

In the early days of libraries books were scarce and expensive and it
was soon found to be necessary to chain them, so they could be studied
but not removed. The Wimborne Chained Library was founded in 1686
by the Rev. William Stone as a free library and now consists of 240
books, many of which are very rare. The books are attached to the
shelves by chain formed of rod-iron bent into a figure of 8 with one end
twisted round the middle for strength. Each chain is about 3ft. long and
has at one end a ring similar to a curtain ring which running along an iron
rod allows considerable play. The chains are fixed to the fore-edges of
the books and are placed back first on the shelves; thus the books can be
placed on a desk but cannot be taken away. The oldest book in the
collection is Anselm's *Opuscula* of 1495.

Places of interest in the Neighbourhood
11. The Ancient Astronomical Clock
14. The Man in the Wall
15. The Leper Hospital

Food and Accommodation
Ample available in Wimborne.

63 Where the Trade Union Movement Started

Position. Tolpuddle
Ordnance Map. Dorchester & Weymouth Sheet 194 1.50000
Map Ref. 7980/9440
Access. Halfway between Dorchester and Bere Regis on the A35.

Note. Trade Unions had been in existence for a long time, the Devon and Somerset Woodworkers being organised as a union in 1717 and by 1750 a considerable number of unions were in existence, but had little power.

In 1830 there was a serious outbreak of rioting and rick and machinery burning in Dorset because the labourers thought the introduction of machinery the principal cause of their low standard of living. In 1833 after a bad harvest the wages for a labourer were 7/- a week, and 6/- a week was proposed for 1834. George Loveless, a labourer and Methodist preacher, formed in December a Tolpuddle lodge of the union whose rules which broke the law by prohibiting any member from divulging any secrets of the union. Loveless and five companions, who used to meet under the large oak tree just outside the church now called the Martyr's Oak, were all arrested and charged with administering an unlawful oath and eventually sentenced to transportation to Australia for seven years. The outcry throughout the country which followed really brought the Trade Union Movement to life and it is generally agreed that Tolpuddle was the birthplace of the modern Trade Union Movement.

The tree where the six met is still there for all to see, as well as the Trade Union Council Memorial Cottages at the west end of the village. At the east of the village is a small chapel relating to the Tolpuddle Martyr's with the inscription on the entrance pillars. "Erected in honour of the faithful and brave men of the village who in 1834 so nobly suffered transportation in the cause of Liberty, Justice and Righteousness and as a stimulus to our own and future generations. George Loveless, James Loveless, James Hammett, Thomas Standfield, John Standfield, James Brine. 'We have injured no man's Reputation, Character Person or Property; we were uniting to preserve ourselves, our wives and our children from utter degradation and starvation.' (George Loveless, defence).''

Places of interest in the Neighbourhood
21. The Remarkable Roof (Bere Regis)
22. The Ancient Hour Glass (Bloxworth)
 3. The Beautiful Church that Hardy Saved (Winterborne Tomson)
66. The Knight with the Yorkist Collar (Puddletown)

Food and Accommodation
Available at Tolpuddle, Bere Regis or Dorchester.

64 The Tithe Tomb

Position. Thornford Church
Ordnance Map. Dorchester & Weymouth Sheet 194 1.50000
Map Ref. 6020/1320
Access. From Cerne Abbas take the A352 as far as Minterne Magna, at this point take the road to Yetminster and from here there is a road leading directly to Thornford.

Note. The Tithe Tomb is just outside the entrance of the church on the right. Here on St Thomas's day Tithe money used to be paid to the vicar who sat by the tomb. The Tithe money was paid into a hollow carved out of the top of the tombstone. The church itself is well worth a visit, as it contains several consecration crosses.

Places of interest in the Neighbourhood
65. The Smallest Church in England (Stockwood)

Food and Accommodation
The village Inn offers excellent food and accommodation can be obtained at Yetminster.

65 The Smallest Church in England

Position. Stockwood
Ordnance Map. Melbury ST50 1.25000
Map Ref. 5910/0690
Access. This church is in a very remote spot indeed, and not easy to find. The best way is to take the road from Dorchester to Yeovil (A37), after passing Grimstone continue on the main road for approx. 8½ miles when you will see on your right-hand-side a sign post for Stockwood. Go straight down this lane for a short distance when you will reach a T junction, turn left here and after a few hundred yards on your right hand side you will see Church Farm. Park the car here, and walk down towards the farm house. Just before the house you will see a path across the fields on your left, take this which leads to a small gate, go over the bridge which leads to the church. The key to the church may be obtained on request from the Farm House.

Note. The church is dedicated to St Edwold, brother of the Anglian King, St Edmund, who was murdered by the Danes in about 870 AD. The church itself appears to be the smallest church in England, being 29¼' x 12¾', total of 400 sq. ft. It is very plain and no longer in use. Its remoteness is perfectly suited to a hermit such as St Edwold.

Places of interest in the Neighbourhood
46. The Mystery of the Lone Pillar at Cross and Hand
      (Minterne Magna)
64. The Tithe Tomb (Thornford)

Food and Accommodation
Dorchester and Yeovil, both have plenty.

66 The Knight with the Yorkist Collar

Position. Puddletown Church
Ordnance Map. Dorchester and Weymouth Sheet 194 1.50000
Map Ref. 7580/9440
Access. On the main road from Wimborne to Dorchester (A35)

Note. St Mary's Church Puddletown is amongst the most beautiful churches in Dorset, and has much to offer the visitor. Most interesting of all is probably the tomb of Sir William Martyn, who died in 1503, although in fact the tomb was made some 30 years before. He is wearing a collar of suns and roses alternatively which was the Yorkist badge, this is still perfectly preserved and dates to the War of the Roses. Examples of these collars are very rare, but there is another on Sir John Carent at Marnhull.

Another interesting thing to observe is the door dividing the church from the Athelhampton Chantry. It opens on to the steps to the Rood-Loft which are in an unusually good state of preservation. In older days a platform stood above the screen which divided the Chancel from the Nave, upon it was fixed the Rood, or Crucifix, on either side were figures of St Mary and St John. From the first day in Lent until the Thursday before Easter a curtain called the Lenten Veil was suspended in front of the Rood. It was only raised at the reading of the Gospel of Psalm Sunday. The two staples (to which chains were added later) from which the Lenten Veil hung may be seen in the roof just outside the Chancel Arch.

Places of interest in the Neighbourhood
21. The Remarkable Rood (Bere Regis)
22. Ancient Hour Glass (Bloxworth)
41. The Red Sign Post (Anderson)
 3. The Beautiful Church the Hardy Saved (Winterbourne Tomson)
63. Where the Trade Union Movement Started

Food and Accommodation
Food available at Public House in Puddletown, accommodation in Dorchester.

67 The Walls Alfred the Great Built

Position. Wareham
Ordnance Map. Wareham Sheet SY88/98 1.25000
Map Reference. 9250/8720
Access. On the banks of the River Frome at the south end of the town stands the medieval church of Lady St Mary and nearby are several car parks. Go down Church Lane which lies to the north of the Church and goes through the Churchyard. At end of lane turn left and after a hundred yards you will see the rampart going north with a path on its crest. Follow along as it turns west until the path is cut by the main road. Cross over here and go up road directly opposite which leads to continuation of

St. Mary's, Wareham, from the south bank of the Frome.

the ramparts which eventually turn southwards to the river.

Note. Wareham is one of the most historic of towns and it is claimed that it has been beseiged more times then any other town in England. It was the scene of frequent fighting between the Anglo-Saxons and Danes and later, Matilda and Stephen. The Walls are believed to have been erected as defences in about A.D. 876 by Alfred the Great; the town was thus defended to East, North and West by the high earth walls and palisades and by the river on the South side. There was probably a stone wall added in the late 10th or 11th century. The Walls are at present badly neglected but it is to be hoped that they will soon be restored.

Places on interest in the Neighbourhood
  4. The Creech Folly (West Creech Hill)
20. The Kimmeridge Folly (Kimmeridge)
60. The Splendid Effigy that Salisbury Cathedral did not want
      (Wareham)

Food and Accommodation
Ample of both in Wareham.

68 The Norman Font with the Strange Carvings

Position. Toller Fratrum Church
Ordnance Map. Dorchester and Weymouth Sheet 194 1.50000
Map Ref. 5790/9750
Access. Take the Dorchester to Yeovil road (A37) as far as Grimstone where you take the A356 to Maiden Newton. After a mile beyond Maiden Newton you will see a sign post on the left-hand-side to Toller Fratum.

Note. Toller Fratum is a small but very beautiful hamlet and consists of a church and a very charming small manor house, now used as a farm, which was built about 1540, together with a few houses.

The Font, which is thought to be mid-12th century, consists of a cylindrical bowl with a deep band of interlacing ornament at the top, moulding immediately below and at the base and between them a series of figures and heads. Many of the figures have their arms stretched upward and on one side three columns support a monster with one head and two bodies.

Note also reset on the inside east wall of the Chancel is a small (17'' x 7'') carved stone, quite clearly showing Mary Magdalene wiping the feet of Christ with her hair. This is believed to be Saxon work of the finest order, well worth a visit.

Places of interest in the Neighbourhood
34. The Dole Table (Powerstock)
53. The Beautiful Tower (Beaminster)

Food and Accommodation
Food available in Maiden Newton, accommodation at Dorchester.

69 The S. S. Collar

Position. Netherbury Church on an effigy of Sir Thomas More
Ordnance Map. Taunton & Lyme Regis Sheet 193 1.50000
Map Ref. 4700/9950
Access. From Bridport take the A3066 road to Beaminster; after leaving
Melplash you will see on your right a road leading to Netherbury.

Note. The S. S. Collar was the collar worn by nobility loyal to the
Lancastrian cause and there are several different explanations as to its
origin. It is believed that the order was founded by John of Gaunt who
gave the S. S. Collar to his nephew Richard II. The earliest example
appears on the effigy of Sir John Swinford who died in 1371. Of the
explanations of the origin of S. S. Collar the most likely explanation is
that the S. S. stands for Sanctus Spiritus (Holy Spirit).

  In Dorset there are three fine examples to be seen, the one to be seen
here at Netherbury, the one at Wimborne Minster on the splendid
memorial to John Beaufort, Duke of Somerset (grandson of John of
Gaunt) and his wife. In this case both Beaufort and his wife wear the
collar. The third example is to be seen in Thorncombe Church where it is
worn by Sir Thomas Brook (1419-20) and his wife Joan (1437) in their
magnificent brass, which is one of the finest surviving in England and
which alone would justify a visit to Thorncombe.

Places of interest in the Neighbourhood
53. The Beautiful Tower (Beaminster)

Food and Accommodation
Ample of both at Bridport.

70 The Magnificent Hammer Beam Roof

Position. Tarrant Crawford Abbey grounds
Ordnance Map. Tarrant ST90 1.25000
Map Ref. 9220/0350
Access. Take the B3082 road from Wimborne via Badbury Rings for 5
miles as far as the True Lovers Knot Inn. Turn left here and drive for
about 1 mile to Tarrant Keynston Church carry on about 300 yards
beyond and park the car in the lay-by on the left. Here is a footpath and
bridleway to Tarrant Crawford about ¾ mile, this leads directly to
Tarrant Crawford Church. Go on past the church for about 100 yards
when you will see on your right hand side a long barn now used as a cow
shed.

Note. This old barn is all that remains of the great Cistercian nunnery of Tarrant Kaines, or Crawford, once one of the wealthiest and most favoured of medieval abbeys. Inside the barn is a magnificent hammer beam roof which has probably stood since the abbey's foundation in about 1200, and whose condition is virtually perfect.

Whilst in the neighbourhood do not fail to visit the small church of Tarrant Crawford with its remarkable wall painting describing the life of St Margaret. Somewhere in the churchyard lie the bodies of Bishop Poore, the builder of Salisbury Cathedral; and a sister of Henry III, Joan, the wife of Alexander II of Scotland.

One of the first books in the English Language was written in Tarrant Crawford Abbey for the nuns shortly after its foundation. It is known as the 'Ancren Riwle' and it lists a set of rules for women who wished to become nuns. It was probably written by Bishop Poore and has been described by experts as one of the most perfect models of simple, natural, eloquent prose in our language.

Places of interest in the Neighbourhood
  1. The Medieval Amplifiers (Tarrant Rushton)

Food and Accommodation
Accommodation available at Wimborne and Blandford. Food available at the True Lovers Knot Inn, Tarrant Keynston.

71 The Judas Tree

Position. Church of Gussage St Andrew
Ordnance Map. Bournemouth Sheet 179 1.50000
Map Ref. 9750/1420
Access. From Blandford take the A354 road to Salisbury, carry on for 6 miles until you reach the Cashmoor Inn. Turn left here at the sign post to Gussage St Andrew, after ½ mile there is a farm on the right called Chapel Farm. Take the lane leading up the side of the farm for about 200 yards, park the car here and climb up the steps into the churchyard.

Note. Gussage St Andrew is the smallest of all the Gussages and indeed is rarely mentioned in guide books. The church is a small building without a tower, but is of great interest. On the wall inside are some 12th century medieval wall paintings in a good state of preservation. They show the passion of Christ and are unusual in that one scene depicts the despairing Judas hanging himself from a tree. This is as far as is known the only depiction of Judas hanging himself to be found anywhere in the British Isles, and as such is truly unique.

Another feature of interest is the tomb under the high altar of a man in the 17th century who is buried north to south instead of west to east, as is traditional, and is given pride of place under the high altar which is most unusual. The inscription reads: "Gulieimus Williams de Woodcotts Generos, extremu suum diem clausit Novemb ye 17th 1725. Aged 100." (Trans. "William Williams of Woodcutts, Gentleman, completed the last of his days November 17th 1725".)

Places of interest in the Neighbourhood
72. The Church that Ninian Comper made Beautiful
    (Wimborne St Giles)

Food and Accommodation
Refreshments available at the Cashmoor Inn or the Anvil at Pimperne. Accommodation at Blandford or Salisbury.

72 The Church that Ninian Comper made Beautiful

Position. Wimborne St Giles
Ordnance Map. Bournemouth Sheet 179 1.50000
Map Ref. 0302/1200
Access. From Wimborne take the B3078 for about 9½ miles until just before the road bends towards Cranborne. There is a turning to the left to Shaftesbury (B3081). ½ mile along this road there is a turning to the left signposted Wimborne St Giles (½) mile.

Note. Wimborne St Giles is a small but very pretty village with the old village stocks still on view. This is the seat of the Earls of Shaftesbury who own St Giles House. The church stands by the very pretty village green just outside the entrance to St Giles House.

The present church was almost entirely rebuilt after a disastrous fire in 1908 which almost gutted the old church. Fortunately at the time of the rebuilding the Earl of Shaftesbury called on the services of Sir Ninian Comper (1864-1960), one of the few architects of genius of his period. Comper was also an expert in stained glass, which he used to tremendous effect in the church, giving its interior all the colour and glory of a medieval church.

It is ironic that the church should have been restored to as near as possible to a Catholic church, when Anthony Ashley-Cooper, the 1st Earl of Shaftesbury, was one of the most anti-Catholic politicians of his day and was largely responsible for the massacre of the Catholics following the Titus Oates plot.

Places of interest in the Neighbourhood
  5. The Folly that Humphrey Sturt Built (Horton)
17. Monmouth Ash (Woodlands)
54. Where the boy king sat under the great oak and touched for the
      King's Evil (Horton)
57. The Cottage Orné (Stanbridge)
58. The Philosopher's Tower (Cranborne/Wimborne road)

Food and Accommodation
Ample available at Cranborne (Fleur de Lys) or Wimborne.

73 Where the Stars and Stripes Began

Position. Church Porch at Steeple
Ordnance Map. Purbeck SY87/97/SZ07 1.25000
Map Ref. 9120/8100
Access. From Corfe Castle take the road to Church Knowle and continue to Steeple (1½ miles).

Note. Steeple consists of a church, a farm house and a Manor House and is in a setting of great beauty. In the porch of the church is a coat of arms cut in stone and this is repeated in scarlet paint on the barrel roof. It is the coat of arms of the Lawrences, a family allied to George Washington's ancestors. George Washington wore their arms on his signet ring, and when he came to design a flag for the newly formed United States he used the arms showing the Stars and Stripes to be seen in this little church. Thus the best known flag in the world began its conception in this remote spot.

Places of interest in the Neighbourhood
37. The Agglestone (Studland)
74. For the Prevention of Vice and Immortality (Swanage)

Food and Accommodation
Ample of both at Corfe Castle. Good food available at 'New Inn' at Church Knowle.

74 For the Prevention of Vice and Immorality

Position. Swanage Town Hall
Ordnance Map. Purbeck SY87/97/SZ07 1.25000
Map Ref. 0300/7880

Note. Immediately north of the Town Hall is a small rectangular structure (10' x 8') with a barrel vaulted ceiling, ashlar walls and stone slated roof. It has a doorway at one end and a tablet inscribed "Erected for the Prevention of Vice and Immorality by the friends of Religion and Good Order A.D. 1803". The door is nail studded and the one small window is fitted with a grille. Just how this tiny building was intended to suppress Vice and Immorality is not clear, but it remains a charming example of an early-nineteenth century lock-up.

Places of interest in the Neighbourhood
37. The Agglestone (Studland)
73. Where the Stars and Stripes Began (Steeple)

Food and Accommodation
Ample of both at Swanage.

75 The Sacred Circle

Position. 6½ miles north of Wimborne on the B3078 to Cranborne
Ordnance Map. Cranborne Sheet SU01 1.25000
Map Ref. 0240/1030
Access. Take the B3078 Wimborne to Cranborne road for 6½ miles. On
the left hand side a ruined church can be seen standing in the centre of a
small earthwork. The site is known as Knowlton Rings and is that very
rare thing, a Sacred Circle.

Note. This was a site of great importance in the Bronze Age, as is proved
by the large number of barrows that surround this earthwork for several
miles. There were originally four circular earthworks at Knowlton, only
one of which is perfect, the others having been destroyed by cultivation.
The two original entrances of the remaining circle are opposite to each
other. The wide ditch is on the inside. The bank is unusually broad and
precise in the encircling enclosure. There is no similarity in its
construction to that of any of the earthworks on Cranborne Chase. Two
of the destroyed rings of Knowlton are practically effaced. They are
merely circular undulations on arable land, but the largest of the four still
suggests its original construction in one place - at the back of New Barn
buildings. Here for a short space both the outer bank and the inside ditch
of the rings are partially discernible. This earthwork has never been
excavated but due to its importance it is high on the list of work to be
undertaken by specialists appointed by the Ministry of Works. It is quite
clearly a religious centre, and possibly equal in importance to
Stonehenge.
  Its importance as a religious centre was a direct challenge to Christian
faith and to destroy its power once and for all the Christians built a
church right in the centre of the circle. A similar arrangement can be
seen at Avebury, but there the Christians did not venture to place the
church in the centre of the ring but just outside. Note the large number of
yew trees in the neighbourhood, always a sign of prehistoric religion.
This tradition was absorbed by the Christians so that many Christian
churchyards still have an avenue of yew trees.
  The village of Knowlton was almost wiped out by the Black Death in
1348 and, as the church had no population to serve, it gradually fell into
disuse, falling finally into ruin in the late-eighteenth century. The
roofless church dates to Norman times but excavation will probably
show that it stood on the site of a much earlier Christian Church.

Places of interest in the Neighbourhood
  5. The Folly that Humphrey Sturt Built (Horton)
54. Where the boy king sat under the Great Oak (Horton)
57. The Cottage Orné (Stanbridge)
58. The Philosopher's Tower (Cranborne/Wimborne road)

Food and Accommodation
Ample at Wimborne or Cranborne (Fleur de Lys)

76 Clouds Hill, a Hero's Hideaway

Position. Bovington, Nr Bere Regis
Ordnance Map. Bere Regis SY89 1.25000
Map Reference. 8240/9090
Access. From Bere Regis take the road to Wool, after 6 miles you will see on your right-hand-side a signpost to Bovington Camp and Tincleton. Take this road for 1.4 miles, when there is a turning to the left signposted Clouds Hill. Turn left here for 100 yards, when you will see the cottage. The cottage is now in the hands of the National Trust, and is open to the public from April - September on Wednesday, Thursdays, Fridays, Sundays and Bank Holidays 2.00 p.m. - 5.00 p.m. October - March on Sundays from 1.00 p.m. - 4.00 p.m.

Note. This cottage was the home of the legendary Lawrence of Arabia whilst serving in the R.A.F. under the assumed name of Aircraftsman Shaw. When he retired from the R.A.F. he settled down to live in this remote cottage and lived here until his death in 1935, following a motorcycle accident, a mile or two away on the road to Bovington Camp. Lawrence who played a very large part in the campaign between the Arabs and the Turks during 1914-18 war, was both an enigma and a man of genius. He lived here in very spartan accommodation with only a couch to lie on, a table to work at, and an armchair. Upstairs in the music room is his gramophone and 800 records. He is buried nearby at Moreton (see under the Grave of a Hero).

Places of interest in the Neighbourhood
18. The Grave of a Hero (Moreton)
23. The Church with the Beautiful engraved windows (Moreton)

Food and Accommodation
None at Moreton, but available at Wool and Bere Regis.

77 The Oldest Door In England

Position. Maiden Newton Church
Ordnance Map. Maiden Newton Sheet SY59 1.25000
Map Ref. 5975/9790
Access. From Dorchester take the Yeovil road A37 for about 5 miles when there is a turning on the left hand side to Maiden Newton (5 miles) and Crewkerne (A356).

Note. The church, which is in the centre of the town, has on the north wall what is thought to be the oldest door in England. The door which has neither lock nor latch, has holes in the stone work on either side for barring the door. It appears to be the original Norman door still hanging on its original hinges. The door appears to have been made from planks of wood placed horizontally one above the other.

Places of interest in the Neighbourhood
34. The Dole Table (Powerstock)
42. The Oldest Homes in Britain (Eggardon)
68. The Early Norman Font with the Strange Carvings (Toller Fratrum)

Food and Accommodation
Food available at the Inn in the village, ample accommodation at Dorchester.

78 The Cresset

Position. Church at Alton St Pancras
Ordnance Map. Cerne Abbas Sheet ST60 1.25000
Map Ref. 6990/0240
Access. From Piddletrenthide take the B3143 from 1¾ miles. Church is on the left side of the road.

Note. Alton St Pancras is a very remote village, so remote that Arthur Mee in his famous county series on Dorset missed the village completely! There is indeed little of note, except the Church and Manor House. The Church was almost entirely rebuilt in 1875 and is of little interest except for the Cresset which is a great rarity. The Cresset is a stone nine light holder, probably of very early date. Each of the hollows was filled with oil and a wick floated on the surface, thus providing a primitive form of artificial light. Cressets were probably quite common before wax and tallow candles were introduced but are now very rare and only two other examples are known in the county. One is in Wool Church (4 lights) and the other in Wareham Church (5 lights).

Places of interest in the Neighbourhood
27. The Crusader's Heart (Mappowder)
39. The Unique Post Box (Holwell)
44. The Rails from the Royal Tomb in Westminster Abbey (Piddletrenthide)
45. The Earliest Use of Arabic Numerals in any church in England (Piddletrenthide)

Food and Accommodation
Available at Piddletrenthide or Sturminster Newton.

79 The Bells of Shaftesbury Abbey

Position. Fontmell Magna Church
Ordnance Map. Shillingstone Sheet ST81 1.25000
Map Reference. 8655/11700
Access. Fontmell Magna is on the A350 Blandford-Shaftesbury road 4 miles south of Shaftesbury. The Church is in centre of village.

Note. The Church was entirely rebuilt in 1843 and a third stage added to the Tower. Six bells were now hung whereas previously there had only been four, all post-Reformation. The two extra were both pre-Reformation, one bearing the inscription ''Intersede Pia pro Nobis Virgo Maria'' and the other ''Ave Maria'', both dating from about 1450 A.D. These bells are almost certainly from Shaftesbury Abbey and the local legend of how they came to Fontmell Magna is as follows: ''At the time of the dissolution of the Monasteries before Henry VIII's men reached Shaftesbury 2 bells were removed from the old Abbey for safe keeping; they were taken by horse and cart and buried near the old Church at East Compton, of which the old tower is still standing; the reason they were brought there was that it was downhill all the way.''

They were found in 1800 by a farmer ploughing and were thought to be from the old tower, but their weight and the tower's design make it impossible. When the Church at Fontmell Magna was rebuilt the bells were acquired to make the ring up to six, but the operation was kept quiet for fear that the question might arise as to who were the legal owners.

Another item of interest is the Cross erected in the Churchyard to Lieutenant Salkeld of the Royal Engineers who won the Victoria Cross during the Indian Mutiny by blowing up the Cawnpore Gate at Delhi, thus allowing the British to recapture the city. Lieutenant Salkeld, son of the vicar of this Church, was killed in the moment of victory.

Food and Accommodation
Ample at Shaftesbury and Blandford

80 The Man who may have been Jack the Ripper

Position. Wimborne Minster Cemetery
Ordnance Map. Bournemouth West Sheet SZ09 1.25000
Map Reference. 0090/9980
Access. The Cemetery is on the right-hand side as the road (B3082) leaves Wimborne for Blandford. In the Cemetery are two chapels and on the ground at the side of the left hand chapel is the simple grave of Montague John Druitt, 1857-1889.

Note. Montague Druitt was the second son of William Druitt, Wimborne's leading surgeon. The Druitts lived at Westfield House which still stands. Montague Druitt was educated at Winchester and Oxford and became a barrister on the Western Circuit and Winchester Sessions. The Jack the Ripper murders are the most famous in the history of crime; they were never solved; countless books have been written about them and solutions offered. Apparently Sir Melville Macnaughten of Scotland Yard was convinced Druitt was the Ripper and on a confidential memo says ''he was sexually insane and from private information I have little doubt but that his own family believed him to ˊ have been the murderer.'' Druitt's mother died incurably insane and Druitt drowned himself in the Thames shortly after the last murder. Apparently the police believed Druitt to be the murderer and considered the Ripper Case closed after Druitt's suicide; certainly the murders ceased and until the police file on Jack the Ripper is opened to the public in 1992 we shall have to wait to see the evidence on which the police thought Druitt to be the Ripper.

Places of interest in the Neighbourhood
11. The Ancient Astronomical Clock (Wimborne)
14. The Man in the Wall (Wimborne)
15. The Leper Hospital (Wimborne)
62. The Chain Library (Wimborne)

Food and Accommodation
Ample available in Wimborne

81 The Man who was buried in his Dining Table

Position. Parish Church, Charmouth
Ordnance Map. Axminster. Sheet S729/39
Map Ref. 3640/9360

Note. On the south wall of the Chancel there is a memorial to the Rev. Edward Bragge who died in 1747. This clergyman was a great trencherman and gourmet, so much so that when dying he told his friends he wished to be buried in the table on which he had eaten so many good meals. His friends honoured his wish by cutting up the table and turning it into a coffin in which he was duly buried in the Church.

Just outside the Church door is the tomb of James Warden, a naval lieutenant who fought in nineteen battles under Hawke, was at the surrender of Bellisle and among the first to land in America on the

outbreak of the War but having survived all these perils was shot dead in a duel in 1792 at the age of 56. Warden quarrelled with his friend and neighbour over the trivial matter of a partridge. The two men met in a field near the Hunters Lodge between Charmouth and Axminster; Warden fired first and his ball passed through his opponent's hat. His opponent then fired and put his ball through Warden's heart and then fled the country.

Places of interest in the Neighbourhood
36. Where the King escaped and the history of England was changed.
40. The Saxon shrine.
69. The S.S. Collar.
53. The Beautiful Tower.
47. The strange story of the Posy Tree.
42. The oldest houses in Britain.
34. The Dole Table.
82. The Rebel who escaped the King's Bayonets.

Food and Accommodation
Ample in Charmouth.

82 The Rebel who escaped the King's Bayonets

Position. Knowle Farm, nr. Beaminster
Ordnance Map. Taunton and Lyme Regis. Sheet 193. 1.50000
Map Ref. 4600/0050
Access. From the centre of Beaminster take the road to Broadwindsor for
½ a mile and then the road to Stoke Abbot, clearly marked. Follow this
for ½ a mile when you will see on the left a white fence and a concrete
road leading up to Knowle Farm. On application at the farmhouse you
will be given the key to the burial ground and shown its position in the
field beyond.

Note. In 1685 James Daniel, a lawyer in Beaminster, joined the Duke of
Monmouth's rising against the lawful king James II. After the defeat at
Sedgemoor, Daniel fled to Beaminster and hid in a chamber in his
house. Hearing that soldiers were coming to find him, he fled the house

and headed west until at Knowle Farm he found a barn, where he concealed himself beneath some straw. Scarcely had he done so when he heard the voices of his pursuers, who having searched his house in Beaminster in vain had been told the probable route he had taken.

The soldiers rushed into the barn and commenced to stab their bayonets into the straw time and time again but somehow always just missing Daniel. At length the search was abandoned and the barn left to the fugitive, whose feelings can well be imagined. When better times for Daniel came some four years later, the first thing he did was to buy the barn and land around it and built a private burial ground so that in time he and his descendants would lie in the exact spot where he believed God had saved him. He lived for some 60 years more, dying at the age of 100.

The neat little graveyard known as Daniel's Knowle stands alone in the fields. It is only 40 ft long by 24 ft wide, surrounded by a hedge of holly and a low stone ivy-covered wall – possibly all that remains of the historic barn – and is entered by two massive iron gates. A weeping willow tree brought from Napoleon's tomb in St. Helena casts a peaceful shade over the spot where in extreme old age the former Rebel came at last to lay his bones on the spot where sixty years before he had escaped the bayonets of the king's men.

Places of interest in the Neighbourhood
53. The Beautiful Tower.
40. The Saxon shrine.
69. The S.S. Collar.
47. The strange story of the Posy Tree.
42. The oldest houses in Britain.
34. The Dole Table.
81. The Man who was buried in his Dining Table.

Food and Accommodation
Ample in Beaminster and Bridport.

83 The Superb Fan Vaulting which Sir Walter Raleigh knew well

Position. Sherborne Abbey
Ordnance Map. Sherborne. Sheet ST.61. 1.25000
Map Ref. 6380/1680
Access. Sherborne is on the main A30 London to Yeovil and on the A352 Dorchester to Sherborne roads. The Abbey is in the centre of the town.

Note. The superb Fan Vaulting, the pride of Sherborne Abbey consists of two sections, the Nave Vaulting and Choir Vaulting. In the Choir Vaulting there are 25 bosses in each bay making a total of 75 in the whole vaulting; they are all of foliage design except for three heraldic-shields in the centre of each bay. The Church Authorities have provided flood lighting for 10p. from a switch placed against the South East Tower Pier and to see the full beauty of the Choir Vaulting, one should not fail to use this facility.

The Nave Vaulting is the chief glory of the Abbey and to view it a large mirror has been provided which enables visitors to study the roof in detail. The bounding ribs of the fans are set back some distance from, instead of meeting at, the central roof ridge as is usual. The resulting space is filled with an intricate pattern of ribs with carved bosses at the principal intersections. The bosses are either foliated or carved with heraldic devices or naturalistic subjects, one of which is a very charming Mermaid. The heraldic shields on the bosses include the rebus of Abbot Ramsam; the Arms of the Abbeys of Sherborne, Milton, Cerne and Abbotsbury; the Arms of Cardinals Morton and Bourchier; the Tudor Roses and the Beaufort portcullis, whilst the initials HE on one boss commemorate the marriage of Henry VII to Elizabeth of York, ending the Wars of the Roses.

Sir Walter Raleigh lived for many years in Sherborne and built the new Sherborne Castle as his home. He loved the town and wished to be buried there. He must have seen the beautiful Fan Vaulting very frequently.

There is much of great interest to see in the Abbey and there are excellent guide books available at the bookstall.

Places of interest in the Neighbourhood
56. The Hiding Place which saved the life of Charles II.
39. The Unique Post Box.
64. The Tithe Tomb.
84. The Alms Houses where Sir Walter Raleigh made a protest.

Food and Accommodation
Ample in Sherborne.

84 The Alms Houses where Sir Walter Raleigh made a protest

Position. Near the entrance to Sherborne Abbey
Ordnance Map. Sherborne. Sheet ST61. 1.25000
Map Ref. 63.85/1655

Note. Close to Sherborne Abbey stand the beautiful Alms Houses called
the Hospital of St. John, open to visitors from Whitsun to the end of
September. The Chapel was completed in 1442 and the whole building a
year or two later, to house "twelve poor feeble and impotent old men and
four old women." In the Chapel is to be seen the famous triptych
probably of the Flemish School c. 1475 and almost certainly made for
the Chapel. At the Reformation it was banished to the old Boardroom
and kept closed and mouldering until the late 19th Century. It has now
been lovingly restored and replaced in its original position; it is a
painting of national importance and was displayed at the Royal Academy
in 1923 in the exhibition of British Primitives. The most moving object,
however, in the Chapel is a letter signed by Sir Walter Raleigh showing a
kinder side to this proud and famous man. It is addressed to the Master
and Brethren about 1593 when Raleigh was at the height of his fame and
power. It reads as follows:

Mr. Knoyll
    This poor woman Elliner Dyer hath been diverse times with me and
Sir Rapf Horsye to complain against the master off the Allmeshows off
Sherburn of the wrongfull retainings off a tenement from her, at such
time as she was a very child when she had no friend to help her, and for
as much as the wrong she Receveth seemeth to be aparaint as myself and
Sir Rapf Horsye are informed and I think you cannot deny, I pray you be
a means to the Rest of Thare Company, that this poor soul may at last
restored to her Ryght and not Driven further to complain against them in
a matter so unjustly begon and persecuted by them that are or should be
protectors and not oppresors off poor pepill wher off I hope you and the
Rest will have due consederacyon with out giving presedent off so great
an ill.

From my Castell this 25th May
Your loving fd.
W. Ralegh.

To my loving ffrend Mr. Edward Knoyll.

We do not know whether the appeal was successful but it is nice to know that Sir Walter could take time off from affairs of State to try and help a friendless old lady. Certainly it is very moving to hold this letter and to bridge four hundred years back to the day when Sir Walter tried to help poor Elliner regain her rights.

Places of interest in the Neighbourhood
39. The Unique Post Box.
56. The Hiding Place which saved the life of Charles II.
64. The Tithe Tomb.
83. The Superb Fan Vaulting which Sir Walter Raleigh knew well.

Food and Accommodation
Ample in Sherborne.

85 The Octagonal House

Position. Nottington near Weymouth
Ordnance Map. Weymouth (North). Sheet S7 68/78. 1.25000
Map Ref. 6620/8260
Access. Take the Weymouth to Dorchester Road A354 for two miles and
turn down road on left marked Nottington. In the centre of the village
opposite the Manor House you will see the three-storied Octagonal
House.

Note. This strange house was built in 1830 as the Spa House for the
Spring whose waters as far back as 1660 were claimed to have great
power to cure all manner of sickness, including Cancer. It was claimed

that a shepherd in 1660 was driving a flock of sheep through the village, many of which were suffering from scab. As he passed the Spring which was next to the road and open, several of the sheep drank the water and as it had formed a small lake or pool, walked through it and washed themselves; such of the flock as did this recovered and became sound which was attributed to the virtues of the water. Over the next two centuries the fame of the water grew and people came from far and wide to seek cures, including George III and his Queen, who came here in June 1791. As the crowds grew there was increasing demand for a proper Spa House, thus in 1830 this house was built over the Spring and at a banquet to celebrate the occasion the owner claimed that he had as his object the benefit of the community far more than any pecuniary consideration. The house is unusual in being octagonal. It has been claimed that the owner had seven sons and built them all a room and one for himself and it is said that in the dining-room there was an octagonal table.

For a full description of the claims of cures and the analysis of the water see the article: Nottingham Spa. Proceedings of Dorset Natural History and Archaeological Soc. Vol 104. 1982. p.19.

The Spring, controlled by a pump, is still to be seen in the basement of the house if the owners are approached. The water smells strongly of Sulphuretted Hydrogen but the taste is not unpleasant.

Places of interest in the Neighbourhood
  7. The Battle in the Pulpit.
  8. The Ancient Stone Cross.
  10. The Altar Stone the Reformers missed.
  33. The man who was buried neither in the Church nor out of it.

Food and Accommodation
Easily available in Weymouth.

86 The Roman Aquaduct

Position. Notton Mill to Dorchester
Ordnance Map. Dorchester S769. Sheet 1.25000
Map Ref. 6700/9130
Access. Take the Bridport road from Dorchester (A35T). After a few yards from the main roundabout at the top of Dorchester's High West Street take the turning on the right just before the barracks. After a mile on the left hand side is Whitfield Farm. Here there is a right of way; walk along this for about a hundred yards when the banks of the Aquaduct are to be seen to either side. The Aquaduct can be followed all the way to Notton Mill.

Note. To ensure an ample supply of water for their new town of Durnovaria the Romans built an aquaduct from Notton Mill near Maiden Newton to Dorchester, a distance of twelve miles and with a fall over the distance of 25 ft. The aquaduct was built as a flat bottomed ditch with steep sides on a ratio of 2:1. In some sections however it was a flat terrace prepared in a natural slope of chalk. Near Whitfield Farm the excavated soil formed an outer bank still well marked. The bottom, which is between 2½ and 3 ft. below the chalk surface, is generally 5 ft. wide. Assuming an average depth of 2 ft., calculations show water would have reached Dorchester at a rate of 13 million gallons a day. There is no evidence that the channel was covered or lined except that where it cut into the filling of the Iron Age Fort of Poundbury the outer side was built up in clay. The construction of this great aquaduct, winding and twisting across the hills and villages for twelve miles shows how greatly the Romans loved water and the efforts they were prepared to make to ensure an ample supply for their fountains, baths and drinking requirements. Obviously there must have been a reservoir to store the water but this has never been traced.

Places of interest in the Neighbourhood
  2. The Norman Tympanum and the Roman Tombstone.
 24. The Church Parson Barnes loved.
 30. The Room where Judge Jefferies held his Bloody Assize.
 61. The Hangman's Cottage.

Food and Accommodation
Ample at Dorchester.

87 Where King Canute died whilst praying at the Shrine of St Edward the Martyr

Position. Shaftesbury Abbey grounds
Ordnance Map. Shaftesbury. Sheet ST 82. 1.25000
Map Ref. 86.40/23.05
Access. The Abbey grounds are to be found down a lane leading off the west end of the High Street. The lane is clearly marked "to Abbey Grounds". The grounds, which overlook a magnificent vista of the beautiful Blackmore Vale are open from Easter to the end of September, seven days a week.

Note. The Abbey was founded by Alfred the Great and the first Abbess was his daughter Aethelgeofe. In due course the Abbey became the largest Benedictine nunnery in England and it was said that if the Abbot of Reading married the Abbess of Shaftesbury they would own all southern England between them.

In AD 979 the body of St. Edward was brought here from Wareham, following his murder at Corfe Castle a year previous, and a shrine built on the north side of the Chancel. In AD 1038 King Canute came to pray at the shrine and died of a heart attack whilst praying; his body was taken to Winchester and buried in the old Minster. At the reformation the nuns of Shaftesbury hid the coffin of St. Edward, leaving only the empty shrine to the fury of the Reformers. In 1931 a roughly made leaden casket was unearthed near the crypt; it contained the fractured bones of a young man and thus corresponds with the record that the King was dragged for a considerable distance with one foot in the horse's stirrup and bruised to death. The relics are now in private ownership – it would be nice to think that one day they may be restored in a shrine in the Abbey where they have rested for over a thousand years.

Places of interest in the Neighbourhood
79. The Bells of Shaftesbury Abbey.

88 Stachy's Well

Position. Ibberton Village. The road from Shillingstone and Oakford Fitzpaine to Ibberton is clearly marked.
Ordnance Map. Bulbarrow Hill. Sheet ST 70. 1.25000
Map Ref. 7890/0770

Note. The search for Stachy's Well takes one into one of the most beautiful villages in all Dorset, Ibberton. Frederick Treves in his delightful *Highways and Byways in Dorset* says of this village 'a jumble of thatched cottages, gardens and orchards lies in a green bay made by a curve in the downs. If the sea could reach it there would be found in the place of the village, a sheltered cove in an amphitheatre of hills. The Church is so high up on the slope that the view from the churchyard extends far beyond the northern limits of the County over the Blackmore Vale. Below the Church a spring breaks out of the rock and finds a way through a thicket of fern and bramble to a well under an aged Yew Tree which bears the local name of Stachy's Well. This does not serve to keep green the memory of some worthy welldigger but commemorates the fact that the well, like the Church, is dedicated to St Eustachius, a Roman General who was martyred for becoming a Christian. The saint's name being inconveniently long, the villages amicably changed it to 'Stachy's'.

The Spring still flows, but alas the Water Board has changed the well to a reservoir and piped the water down to the village, where from a tap opposite the pub one can still drink the pure spring water from the Saint's Well – as people here have done in this enchanted place for over a thousand years.

Places of interest in the Neighbourhood
27. The Crusader's Heart.
39. The Unique Post Box.

Food and Accommodation
Good pub meals at Anstey and Oakford Fitzpaine. Accommodation at Milton Abbas and Blandford.

89 The Little Huguenot who became the Lady of the Manor

Position. Little Bredy.
Ordnance Map. Dorchester and Weymouth. Sheet ST 194. 1.50000
Map Ref. 5780/8900

Note. The village of Little Bredy lies in a beautiful fold of the hills and is worth a visit for its setting alone. At the centre is Bridehead, set in a splendid park and bordering a lake: all around are gentle green hills and to one side is a cricket field. The house was largely rebuilt in 1847 but charmingly so in the Strawberry Hill Gothic style, though on the north side some 16th century work is to be seen.

In the little church is a memorial which reads:

"Sacred to the memory of Jane youngest daughter of Francis Chassereau Esquire formerly of Niort in France.
An exile at the age of fourteen to this country in consequence of the revocation of the Edict of Nantes.
and relict of the late Robert Williams Esq of Moor Park Herts and of Bridehead in this parish representative in Parliament for the Borough of Dorchester. She died on the 8th October 1841 at the age of 102 years the mother, grandmother and great grandmother of a numerous family who remember with love, reverence and gratitude her pure faith and simple piety, her unbending integrity, her excellent sense, her childlike cheerfulness, her affectionate readiness to help, to forgive and to comfort all around her."

Unfortunately owing to lack of punctuation a wrong impression is given. It was not Jane who fled from France aged fourteen, but her father. Jane was born in 1739 in London, where her father was a shopkeeper to the Huguenot community. After her marriage to Robert Williams she became lady of the manor at Moor Park, and did not move to Bridehead until nearing her century.

Places of interest in the Neighbourhood
2. The Norman Tympanum and the Roman Tombstone
30. The Room where Judge Jefferies held his Bloody Assize
31. The Flying Angel
61. The Hangman's Cottage

90 Dame Elisabeth Frink's beautiful memorial to the Dorset Martyrs

Position. Dorchester. At the junction of South Walks and Icen Way.
Ordnance Map. Dorchester, Sheet SY69 1.25000
Map Ref. 6980/9050
Access. Ask any local to direct you to South Walks and follow along until you see the statues at the junction with Icen Way.

Note. The sixteenth and seventeenth centuries were times of great religious upheaval with the Protestants gaining power and seeking to eliminate the Catholic Faith. To this end the most severe Penal Laws were introduced whereby it was death by hanging, drawing and quartering for being a priest, for attending Mass, sheltering a priest, distributing Catholic books and for sending children abroad to receive a Catholic education. This persecution to death lasted from 1545 to 1684. The Catholic resistance in Dorset was based on the great catholic families, the Arundels of Wardour Castle, the Welds of Lulworth and Chideock, the Webbs of Canford and the Jesuit College at Stapehill.

Throughout the period Priests and layfolk continued to lay down their lives in a most barbarous and painful way on this spot. In these days of religious tolerance it has been thought proper to remember these brave people and in 1978 a committee was formed to see what could be done. In 1981 the Arts Council gave a grant of £9,000 and the total cost of £38,000 was donated by private subscribers and Dame Elisabeth Frink was commissioned to provide the beautiful life and a quarter size statues. The figures illustrate two of the Martyrs submitting themselves humbly to the Mediaeval figure of Death in the form of the hangman. There is a simple plaque "For Christ and Conscience Sake" and a list of those Dorset men who suffered here. John Speed's map of Dorchester 1610, shows this to be the exact spot of execution. Those commemorated here are: St. Alexander Briant S.J., executed 1st December 1581; John Slade, executed 30th October 1583; Thomas Hemerford, executed 30th October 1584; John Munden, executed 12th February 1584; John Adams, executed 8th October 1586; Thomas Pilcher, executed 21st March 1587; John Hambley, executed Easter 1587; William Pike, executed Easter 1591; St. Eustace White, executed 10th December 1591; William Pattenson, executed 22nd January 1592; John Cornelius S. J., executed 4th July 1594; Thomas Bosgrave, executed 4th July 1594; John Carey, executed 4th July 1594; Patrick Salmon, executed 4th July 1594; Hugh Green, executed 19th August 1642; also William Warmington, banished January 1585; John Jessop, Died in Dorchester Gaol 1588; Helen Tremain, Died in Dorchester Gaol 1588; ... Morecock, Died in Dorchester Gaol before 1591; and many others of all persuasions whose names are not recorded.

Places of interest in the Neighbourhood
30. The room where Judge Jefferies held his Bloody Assize (Dorchester)
61. The Hangman's Cottage (Dorchester).

Food and Accommodation
Ample available in Dorchester

91 Henry III and the White Hart

Position. Kingstag
Ordnance Map. Sturminster Newton. ST71 1.25000
Map Ref. 72.50/1060
Access. Take B3143 northward from Piddletrenthide to Pulham and
continue on for 1½ miles to Kingstag. Here just past "The Green Man"
Public House is a small bridge over the River Lydden.

Note. The legend goes that Henry III while out hunting near here came
across "a beautiful and goodly white hart". So moved was he by the
comeliness of the startled creature that he spared its life and forebore
to follow it save with his eyes. Sometime later Sir Thomas de la Lynde,
Bailiff of Blackmore Forest, came across the same white hart and,
unmoved by its beauty, turned on it and after a chase killed it at the
foot of this bridge. When Henry III heard of this he was so enraged that
he seized Sir Thomas and his companions, cast them into prison and
fined them very heavily. Such, furthermore, was his sorrow at the loss
of the stag that he laid a tax upon the land its feet had trod. Thus for
many years "white hart silver" was paid by squire and yeoman into the
exchequer and the Vale of Blackmore became known as the Vale of the
White Hart. Many doubts have been cast on the story but there is no

doubt a tax called White Hart Silver was levied since writing three hundred years later Thomas Fuller tells us "Myself hath paid a share for the same who never tasted meat". Moreover we have the bridge still called Kings Stag Bridge and the hamlet of the same name nearby. The best view of the bridge is from the field on the right hand side.

Places of interest in the Neighbourhood
78. The Cresset
27. The Crusader's Heart
39. The Unique Post Box
44. The Rails from the Royal Tomb in Westminster Abbey
45. The Earliest Use of Arabic Numerals in any Church in England

Food and Accommodation
Good food is obtainable at many of the village Inns. Accommodation at Dorchester and Piddletrenthide.